The Coat and
The Crucifix

The Coat and The Crucifix

David Thompson

THE CHOIR PRESS

First published in the United Kingdom in 2024 by
The Choir Press

ISBN 978-1-78963-483-9

Contents

Preface

Of the general historicity of the story of Joseph there seems to be no doubt. Allowance may be made for the long period that elapsed before the traditions were reduced to writing in their present form, and for the tendency to project the characteristics of a tribe backwards into some imaginary hero. But the incidences are too natural for and too closely related to be entirely a product of fiction; and the Egyptian colouring, which is common to both the principal documents, is fatal to any theory that resolves the account into a mere elaboration in a distant land of racial pride. Joseph's character as depicted shows no traces of constructive art but is consistent and singularly attractive. Dutifulness is perhaps a keynote, manifested in the resistance to temptation, in uncomplaining patience in misfortune, and in the modesty in which he bore his elevation to rank and power. Instead of using opportunities for the indulgence of opportunities for resentment, he recognises the action of Providence and nourishes the brothers who had lost all brotherly affection for him. On the other hand, there are blemishes which should never be exaggerated or overlooked. In his youth there was a degree of vanity, that made him rather unpleasant company. That his father was left so long in ignorance of his safety in Egypt may have been unavoidable but leaves a suspicion of inconsiderateness. On the whole a very high place must be given him among the early founders of his race. In strength of right purpose, he was second to none, whilst in the graces of reverence and kindness of insight and assurance, he became the type of a faith which is at once personal and national and allows neither misery nor a career of triumph to eclipse the sense of divine destiny.

R. W. Moss
Hastings Dictionary of the Bible 1909

Introduction

Although Joseph lived more than three thousand five hundred years ago the story of his life speaks to us today. He was fully human yet flawed, passionate but principled, merciful but righteous. Above all he faithfully walked with God. God was with him and in him. Such is the vividness of the account of his life that we feel not a whisker separates us from him. His story was handed down by word of mouth until the final version was edited possibly between the fifth and seventh century BC. The story of Joseph is a story of redemption. It is true because it's true, because it's true, not because it was written on tablets of stone. I remember Professor Nineham saying that tales told from the American civil war, although legendary, retain a kernel of truth. The legends were not pure fiction but based on real events. Moreover, the arresting but divergent Gospel accounts of the resurrection point to their veracity. We may not be sure how many angels were present but are left in no doubt that the tomb was empty. Nor are we left in any doubt that Joseph was a man whose heart God had touched. Equally he was a cocky youth with a coat of many colours who, following a chain of disastrous events, was purified in the refiner's fire. Curiously we learn nothing about how, when or where he prayed. So anything I say about how he felt, thought or prayed in the following pages is pure supposition. That he was a living prayer, however, is to be seen in the manner of his living.

I make no apology for recounting significant moments from my early years for without them the link with Joseph makes no sense. When I was five years old, after gazing out of the window while lying in bed at the end of the war, I was suspended in God's love and given a glimpse of my future life. This was followed by a dream about Joseph and his dreams. It seemed that he was to be the key to my understanding of what had been made known. As I write these words I can see a crucifix on the wall given to me at my confirmation as a reminder of Christ's glorious victory over sin, death and the opening of the gates of heaven. The same crucifix hung above my bed in the Central YMCA in London in 1960. Spotted by a friend, I was invited to serve at St George's Church Bloomsbury, then the London University church. This changed everything and paved the way for ordination. Joseph was my mentor. He never ever wanted to be a hero, or become a celebrity, he just wanted to be Joseph. This is why he is so attractive. He wasn't pushy but grew in humility. He wasn't a power seeker but content to serve at home, in prison or as grand vizier.

David Thompson   Pentecost 2024

CHAPTER 1

The Coat

THE LIVING GOD

God is the same yesterday, today and for ever. A thousand years in his sight are but a watch in the night. A slither of time separates us from Joseph who was always aware of the presence of the living God. As a child I already knew about Joseph because my mother had read the Joseph stories. At that time we were living in Woodhouse Manor farm in the Yorkshire Dales, where we had been evacuees since the Blitz. The handsome farmhouse encircled by the fells was a landmark not far from the river Wharfe. Lying in bed I could hear the beck skipping and dancing down the valley to be swallowed up by the fast-flowing river Wharfe a few fields away. One night I was gazing through the bedroom window at orange-tinted brown clouds floating past a watery full moon. The next moment I was caught up in the love and mercy of my Heavenly Father. I heard nothing, I saw nothing. But in the security of God's love I was given a glimpse of the whole of my life from innocent childhood deep into old age. It unfolded before my eyes like a panoramic film. It was what is called an intellectual vision. I heard nothing, I saw nothing, but I was simply made aware of what lay ahead. For this reason I will try to express, eighty years later, what was wordlessly made known to me as a little child. There were two parts to the call. The first about my family and the second about my vocation. It also included fleeting glances of specific times of trial. Although I was addressed as if I was spiritually adult, I was aware that some things were withheld because too difficult for a child to understand. Following this disclosure my attention was drawn to the story of Joseph and his dreams. It was to be the key to my further understanding of what I had been shown. Over the years the pinch points became clear. In God's good time a calling to prayer and to the ordained ministry were drawn to my attention by priests.

The never-ending summer of 1947 was unforgettable. It was a summer which seemed to last for ever. It was a dream-like summer when flocks of Clouded Yellow butterflies flew across from Africa and adorned the lucerne fields behind our home. In our own back garden we also saw hosts of Brimstones, Red Admirals, Peacocks, Commas, Orange tips, Painted Ladies, Tortoiseshells and an array of butterflies in quantities I don't think I have ever seen since. It must have been in the early summer that I had been unwell. While convalescing I took a few steps out of the sun porch into a verdant garden. Quite suddenly I found myself standing stock still, rooted to the spot. It was as if I had a new pair of eyes. I saw the garden transfigured – charged with the glory of God. Throughout my childhood years I had never been in doubt about the presence of God in the natural world. That panenhenic moment, however, remains deeply imprinted on my mind.

Shortly after I began preparing for ordination I was standing outside Woodlands, East Acklam, our cottage home in the Yorkshire Wolds with Harold Gill, the tenant farmer in Woodhouse Manor farm and my proxy father during the war years. After precious shared silence, as he gazed at the sky, he told me that he knew someone or something was out there for whom he clearly held a deep respect. As a man who seldom darkened the doors of the church these were words of encouragement and support. As I considered the way he stood in silence at the gate on the farm looking out across the fields and up at the clouds above Simon's seat I was hardly surprised that he had given me such a blessing.

THE WORD WAS MADE FLESH

While a student reading theology at Kings College London I had a moment of insight about the miracle of the incarnation. Wearied with my studies in Dr Williams library, reading about the Finnish sleeping preachers, I walked down the road to the Church of Christ the King, Gordon Square. It was by then the London University church. Sitting close to the North wall in the vast open space of Pugin's majestic masterpiece I found myself reading St John Chapter 6. My befuddled mind wrestled with the words 'I am the bread of life.' Suddenly the words came alive. My heart and soul apprehended what my mind couldn't fathom. Somehow, I knew that the risen Lord was close. I saw nothing. I heard nothing. But for a few moments I sensed that I was no longer alone. So this is what my great-uncle Canon Francis Mercer meant, when he said, 'There are many things about which I am no longer sure but of one thing I am absolutely certain, the presence of the living risen Christ.' From then on, I knew that the resurrection of Christ was so much more than a historical event or an interesting idea but a living, present, universal reality.

THE BREATH OF LIFE

As I grew up, childhood memories of God's loving presence were retained. In my youth I didn't spend hours in private prayer but was schooled in the Bible. Daily chapel fuelled my soul with hymns and psalms. Confirmation classes when I was fifteen in which we learned the catechism by heart opened my eyes to the need to work at prayer. Shortly before I left school I was called in by my housemaster, who listed various suitable occupations before suggesting I consider ordination. An icy chill went down my spine. Genteel poverty didn't appeal. When told that we had never had it so good by the Prime Minister in the late nineteen-fifties I was excited by the prospect of doing my own thing. Three years later, on my twentieth birthday, I awoke in the slough of despond but could see no way of escape. One Sunday morning, when everyone was on holiday and the cold damp streets of London were deserted, soulless and empty, I hit rock bottom. Everything was closed apart from the Lyons Corner House across the road. It too was empty. Somehow I had lost my way. I had begun to feel as lonely in a crowd celebrating New Year's Day in Trafalgar Square as on that bleak soulless Sunday. Shortly after this the crucifix on the wall in my room in the Central YMCA came to the rescue. Noticed by Roger Harley through the open door of my room, it led to an invitation to St George's Church Bloomsbury, where I briefly met Father Ivor Smith Cameron. Later on that same year, on a dull, damp, dark November evening, he rang me up. When I responded to the call to go to the phone booth I was surprised to find that he was on the other end of the line. I hardly knew him. Moreover, there was such a noise that it was difficult to hear what he had to say. What I heard was, 'David, when are you going to be a priest?'

I was electrified. Immediately I knew that this was what was missing. In an attempt to pull myself together I slowly ascended the grey stone steps to the empty chapel on the first floor, where I knelt to pray. For forty minutes I didn't know where to put myself as my lips took off on their own. My body shook, and I found myself praising God in what seemed to be an incomprehensible language. Deeply moved by the Holy Spirit, I was beside myself with joy. This was it. This is what I had been looking for. The sacrifices that I would now be called to make seemed trivial. Moreover, the word sacrifice itself took on a new meaning. Quite simply it meant that I was to say a wholehearted yes to God and prepare myself to second his proposals. In order to clear the way for this journey there were things to do. I had played hockey at County level. It was too expensive and time-consuming. This had to go. I didn't pursue a completed application form to enter the Royal Academy of Music, so flute and trombone were put on the shelf. More costly was the discovery that, once accepted for ordination training, I would be expected to break up with my girlfriend. Permission to marry would not have been granted until a second curacy. In the event this would have been ten years. Having made such moves in the following decade and happily married I became complacent. I failed to notice pride slip in through the back door. My innocent desire for sporting success as a teenager had been replaced by an unhealthy desire for academic success. After I was ordained, two or three posts for which I had been recommended didn't materialise. God in his love and mercy gently wrested these trophies from my grasp. It was only after being stripped of such ambitions that I finally came to terms with the call to stay faithfully on course as a parish priest.

TRIALS

Day by day watching boys from his father's school go to war and never come back while awaiting his own turn left its mark on my father. A photograph of him in his Officers' Training Corps uniform reveal a sad emaciated figure. Shortly after the First World War he was seriously ill and stayed in bed for a year. After the Second World War he suffered from depression. My twin brother had a traumatic birth and was later diagnosed as suffering from schizophrenia and autism. There was a time when it wasn't safe for him to stay at home. My older son with learning difficulties was diagnosed with schizophrenia when he was nineteen. As I ponder these things I recall that when Abraham sent Hagar away, she was desperate. The water had run out and Ishmael was crying.

'God heard the child crying and the angel of God called to Hagar from heaven and said, "Don't be afraid." Then he opened her eyes and she saw a well of water. So Hagar went and filled the skin with water and gave the boy a drink.'

One Christmas Eve I was desperate. My twin was missing. My

parents had left home because they didn't feel safe. I travelled to Harrogate by train to join them in a hotel for Christmas. On seeing their distress, I went to my room to deposit my suitcase and fell down on my knees, asking for help. The response to my pleas was direct. *Don't you think I love him much more than you do.*

Moments such as these helped me spiritually to keep on carrying on and to remember that God was with me and in me. If sloth was the enemy which tempted me to throw in the towel and pride was over concerned about success it was circumstance which providentially directed me down paths I never planned to tread. The first, the call to prayer and ordination, the second, the call to leave home, family and parish to pray.

THE COAT OF MANY COLOURS

The night after the blackout curtains were removed I was directed to the story of Joseph. In the following pages I consider why his story was drawn to my attention. Before I went to school my mother had given me what she called my coat of many colours. Clothing coupons didn't go far in the war years, so it was made up from an old tweed jacket belonging to my godfather, David Bungey. Before he went to Canada to train as a pilot, he was staying with my family in Writtle in the early days of the war. By the time I put on my coat of many colours he was serving as a navigator on a Lancaster bomber. For many years I never spoke a word about the coat, the showing, or the significance of the story of Joseph. Moreover, it never occurred to me that my mother had any idea of the significance of the restyled tweed jacket. No doubt it was made for me rather than my twin because it had once belonged to my godfather. But maybe she did! Shortly before we were married, she led Philippa to the top of the tall garden in Avening, which was by then our family home in Gloucestershire. There she advised her that she would have to share me with God.

She also spoke to her about the way that serving officers had to be prepared to leave home and family to serve overseas as her father had done as an officer in Normandy during the First World War. It hadn't been easy for her. Her father never fully recovered after the war. My grandmother told me that she couldn't go to sleep until after he had come unsteadily upstairs and the candle had been extinguished. He died nine years later of peritonitis. He was just 47.

*

THE INHERITANCE OF JOSEPH

Joseph was a child when his mother Rachel died, leaving Jacob broken-hearted. By the time he was given a coat of many colours he had inherited the faith of his fathers. Both his great-grandfather, Abraham, Isaac his grandfather, and his father Jacob knew that amidst a diversity of beliefs was to be found the living God. Although the book of Genesis says little about the theology of Joseph or his prayer both are writ large in his devoted Godly living. He worshipped the same God Father, Son, and Holy Spirit whom we worship today. When Jacob his father said, 'Surely God is in this place,' he was speaking about the God and Father of us all. A slither of time separates us from Jacob. A thousand years in God's sight is but a watch in the night. Centuries come and go. Each flies forgotten as a dream dies in the opening day.

CHAPTER 2

The Pit

SETTING OUT

At the age of seventeen, when the sun began to set over the Judean hills, Joseph could dream dreams and look upon a world charged with the glory of God. This is where he experienced the joy of the nursery slopes before being led to more testing terrain. Home life in Hebron was good. Joseph was the favourite son of Jacob, not only because he was Rachel's first-born but because he was gracious, talented and favoured by God and man. This comfortable existence came to an abrupt end when he set out on a costly journey of faith in which he was to learn the significance of his dreams.

The die was cast when Jacob called Joseph aside to ask him to go to Schechem to find his brothers. From the moment he set out he never went home. Dothan was sixty miles from Hebron, so the journey would take several days. His chosen route might have followed the way along the valleys to Schechem, which was a no go area because of the terrible crimes of his brothers. More likely he selected the ridge route on higher ground which ran alongside the Judean and Samarian hills. Once on the way he began to feel a spring in his step as he walked along the lower slopes of the hills and found himself wondering at the miracle of creation. At the end of the day his feet were sore. As he drew nearer to Schechem his muscles cramped. During the night he found himself thinking about his dreams. He was still troubled by the anger of his brothers. It was over the top. He was also puzzled and disturbed by his father's frosty reaction. At the dawn of each new day, he cheered up. He had always taken one day at a time, placing his trust in God, and had learned about the faith of the God of Abraham from Jacob and Rachel. This belief included a simple knowing that the family of Jacob was called to play an important part in the service of God. On approaching Schechem Joseph began to worry about the ever-increasing hostility of his brothers. They already knew that the first-born son of Jacob's beloved Rachel, their half-brother, held a special place in their father Jacob's heart and simmered with envy. His dreams had made things a whole lot worse. It was while he was sharing his first dream that he realised he was pouring fuel on the flames. For Joseph had openly shared this dream with all his brothers.

'We were binding sheaves of corn in the field,' he told them, 'when suddenly my sheaf stood upright while your sheaves gathered round and bowed down.'

Being in the fields at harvest time was something I experienced as a child. Memories of the sweet smell of hay enabled me to envisage life on Jacob's farm. But all was not well. His brothers were outraged that Joseph might one day lord it over them. Nevertheless, so long as Jacob was at home Joseph felt safe. The second dream included Jacob. For Joseph dreamt that 'The sun, the moon and eleven stars were all bowing down to him.' This he shared with the whole family.

His father was testy, saying, 'Do you really believe that your father and mother and brothers will one day bow down and worship you?'

As Joseph approached the hostile territory of the Schechemites he lost his way. After walking around in circles in the heat of the day he became disorientated. With only a vague idea about where to go he bumped into a man who gave him directions. There was something about him which puzzled Joseph. He was extraordinarily gracious and humble. He looked like a man but when Joseph turned around to thank him – a fleeting glance – and then the man was nowhere to be seen. As he stared into empty space he found himself thinking about the appearance of three men to his great-grandfather Abraham and wondered if the man might have been a messenger sent from God, steering him away from the dangers of the hostile men of Schechem and providentially towards the place where his brothers might be found on a hillside tending the sheep. Having never seen an angel he thought it must be a man. But as he thought about it, he began to think it was an angel after all. It was some way from where he met the man to the hill of Dothan, so he didn't go far before settling down for the night close to the main highway from Damascus to Egypt and, wearied by his travels, slept like a log.

THE PIT

Having seen no-one for days the brothers of Joseph were surprised to see the approach of a vaguely familiar figure through the haze. Even though wearing his coat of many colours it was a while before they were certain that it was a weary Joseph. They could hardly believe their eyes and wondered what he was up to. As he drew closer and they were sure it was him, their resentment boiled over and they began scheming how best to rid themselves of the first-born son of Rachel and his foolish dreams. No sooner had Joseph dropped down beside them, exhausted, than they beat him up and hurled him down a pit. At the bottom of a manky midden, although dazed and confused, he could just hear Reuben lamely trying to calm his brothers down. Joseph didn't fight back. First of all, it was pointless, and in any case, he didn't hate his brothers. Why should he be demeaned, he wondered, by imitating their brutish behaviour. By restraint he won the moral victory. Further, at no point for the rest of his life did he ever seek for revenge. How long his brothers argued about what to do with him we have no idea but when a caravan of Ishmaelites came along Judah had a brainwave; *if we sell him into slavery we won't have committed murder but will have found the perfect solution.* After handing him over and pocketing the twenty pieces of silver they smeared his precious coat with blood. On their return they told Jacob a fanciful tale about finding Joseph's blood-stained coat as evidence that he had been killed by a wild beast. While being transported to Egypt Joseph was thankful for the miracle that he was still alive but concerned about what might become of him. Nevertheless, there were long periods throughout the best part of the three weeks that it took to travel to Egypt that he learned to contain his soul in patience. Throughout the 250-mile journey he became ever more aware that God was with him. At night he dreamed about the family farm. By day his mind spun with regrets. *If only I hadn't told my father about my brothers' evil ways. If only I hadn't spoken to my family about my dreams. If only I hadn't wound up my brothers.* At times he was sorrowful; at times past caring, but he knew he wasn't alone. As they journeyed across the sand he began to consider that his plight was a wake-up call. Humbled, he began to acknowledge his faults and failings. It was true that the way his brothers had cruelly treated him was outrageous. But was he partly to blame by taking delight in boasting and needling them? Facing the truth and acknowledging his mischief cleared the way for a deeper intimacy with God. In the slave market he was bundled into a crowd of misery but was fortunate to be sold to Potiphar, the captain of the guard, who quickly saw his potential. In this way Joseph found himself in a situation in which his personal gifts, management abilities and wisdom were soon recognised and so, after a series of promotions, he would be appointed Potiphar's right-hand man in charge of all his household. It was while working for Potiphar that he learned how to become all things to all men. He learned how to be an Egyptian amongst the Egyptians. Throughout these years his dreams never ceased to be the glimmer of light at the end of a long tunnel.

*

Dreams are sourced from many seams. They might be products of the human mind, creations of the human subconscious, which itself might be penetrated by data from the collective subconscious. God, however, is with us and in us and might use these or any other channels to make his loving purposes known. Significant dreams aren't easily forgotten. There is something for us to face up to; something for us to do; something for us to see. Joseph, in the Gospel account of the nativity of Jesus, was told not to fear to take Mary as his wife. On the roof top in Joppa St Peter saw a sheet come down from heaven and was commanded to break free from convention in order to preach the Gospel to the Gentiles. Dreams and visions are a gateway to a different kind of seeing and knowing. I once had a warning dream. It was about a steam train clattering along at a recklessly dangerous speed through verdant green fields. As I looked, I saw that I was the engine driver, wearing a dark engine driver's cap. The dream I understood to be a call to slow down. The dreams of Joseph helped him to keep on carrying on. This was important, because his calling had implications for countless other people and spanned a number of years from life on the family farm to retirement in Goshen. Moreover, his story has encouraged people for many centuries and is as relevant today as ever.

LOST AND FOUND

At seventeen I wanted to leave school. Shortly after this I made a hasty decision to become an articled clerk to a chartered accountant in York. Somehow I managed to lose God. It wasn't deliberate. In losing God I also lost touch with the person I was called to be. I remained in the doldrums for a year until I thought I saw an easy escape route. An opportunity was provided by the manager of a branch of the Midland Bank in Leeds. On hearing that I was bogged down in a dark back office he suggested I moved to banking. This, I thought, was to be my passport to freedom. As soon as I could, after basic training in Leeds, I requested and was granted a transfer to a branch in London. There I served in the Midland Bank in Tottenham Court Road, thinking that this was to be the highway to success, wealth, and prosperity. I vividly remember being dropped off at York station with a brown leather suitcase which had belonged to my great-uncle Francis. I had already begun to cut loose from my moorings soon after my father became bankrupt in 1956. Intoxicated by the false confidence of youth I had begun to think that I could go it alone. So when my housemaster looked directly at me as I stood to attention before his desk and said, 'Ordination?' I didn't want to know. Like Jonah, I headed off in the opposite direction as fast as possible. But after a honeymoon period I began to fear that by leaving home and going to London I had burnt my boats. On the surface I was cheerful. None of my family or friends could see that I was struggling. A good job, a good future, living in London – what more did I need. I was beginning to lose hope when ordination cropped up again three years later. It struck a chord. I saw at once that pride had got the upper hand. I had been distracted by wanting to do my own thing. Moreover, I realised that ordination answered the very questions I was for ever asking. What is the meaning of life? What shall I do? Where am I going? What does God require of me? This time my response was freely given. Yes, a thousand times yes. Released from a midden of my own making I was ready to change direction. My friend with whom I shared a room recently told me that I became a different person. My joy was tangible. My heart was free. So it was that I studied for two years before going to Kings College London, where I was privileged to be tutored by Professor Eric Mascall. He helped me to find my way amongst the troubled musings of theologians in the 1960s and flourish on more solid ground. Theological college and liturgical studies supervised by Dr F. L. Cross in Oxford followed. Today as I write I can still see the sunlight shining on the marble floor of Birmingham Cathedral as I stood and read the words of St Luke's Gospel during my ordination as a priest. 'Pray ye therefore the Lord of the harvest that he would send out labourers into his harvest.'

*

What became of Joseph when raised from the pit was a willingness to speedily come to terms with divine providence, knowing full well that God was with and in him.

CHAPTER 3

Prison

ENSLAVED

As Joseph braced himself to cope with whatever awaited, his confused mind began to clear. He knew that things were never going to be the same again. His life as a slave probably began on the bottom rung of the ladder. Very soon his gifts, talents, and loving service were noted so that over a number of years he reached what he must have considered the summit of his career. Joseph was no ordinary slave. He worked hard not just for his own sake nor simply to please Potiphar. He worked for the greater glory of God. During over a decade in slavery Joseph was content to be clay in the potter's hands, being melted and moulded for what lay ahead. Potiphar himself noted 'that the Lord was with Joseph and that the Lord caused all that he did to succeed in his hands'. This is why he was eventually put in charge of Potiphar's entire household. Joseph was vulnerable in many ways, not least because of his former occupation as a shepherd, his race, his success, and because he was handsome in form and appearance. At what he might have considered to be the pinnacle of his career he fell from grace, after being caught napping by Potiphar's wife.

'Lie with me,' she said.

This was not a one-off incident but happened over and over again. Her attentions were persistent and alluring, but he wouldn't listen and tried to keep her at arm's length. Whenever Potiphar wasn't around, she would try to seduce him. Joseph kept his distance, both because of his moral integrity and also because he was a trusted servant. Then one day she found him alone and got hold of him. As he tried to escape, she clung to his coat. When an angry and tearful wife tells Potiphar that Joseph has assaulted her and shows him Joseph's coat as proof of his wrongdoing, an irate Potiphar casts him into his gaol. The contrast with the glory of Potiphar's palace was a sickening blow. Not for the first time, Joseph was reminded that what matters most is not what others think or say but what is good, true and honourable. He consoled himself with the thought that if there is any truth in a complaint it is good to be humble, learn lessons, seek forgiveness and make amends. If baseless to take no notice. He hadn't forgotten that all of his brothers couldn't believe that he had reported their slaying of the men of Schechem to their father Jacob in private, not to make mischief, but for their own good.

PRISON

Had Joseph not faced God he might have emerged from prison a broken man. From the glory of being in charge of Potiphar's household Joseph could hardly have sunk lower than residing in Potiphar's prison. In spite of this humiliation, Joseph continued to walk with God. Hope, faith and love kept him going. Whenever tempted to wallow in misery about the way he had been unjustly treated, he found solace in humble prayer. In spite of the Canaanite culture in which he was surrounded in Hebron in his youth, and the different religious beliefs and practices of the Egyptians, he continued to place his faith in the living God of Abraham, Isaac and Jacob. Throughout his stay in Egypt, he took care not to be sidetracked by superstition. He wasn't beguiled by the trendy focus on numerous deities and countless rituals. Nor was he fooled by surroundings teeming with magicians and spiritual guides. Day by day his faith in the living God increased. In the midst of confusion, he held fast to what he had learned about the faith of his great-grandfather Abraham. Joseph understood that it was Abraham's experience of the living God which had inspired him to go out, not knowing where he was going. It was Abraham's faith which enabled him 'to remain in the land of promise, living in tents with Isaac and Jacob, the heirs with him of that same promise.' When Joseph considered these promises he held on to the belief that in spite of all that was going on he had a calling to play in the destiny of his people. He realised that he was not only a stranger in a foreign land, but a man set apart. Somehow, deep within, he knew that God was working all things together for good. The evidence for the increase of his faith and hope is to be seen in the kind of man he became. It was while in gaol that his soul was prepared for the costly ministry which lay ahead – to feed the hungry as minister of supplies for the whole of Egypt as well as further afield; to forgive and be reconciled with his wayward brothers; and to prepare a home for the family of Jacob in Egypt. The years that Joseph spent in prison weren't wasted. It was there he learnt 'that the darkness is no darkness with thee but that the night is as clear as the day.' While sharing the indignities of the poor and downtrodden his dreams were the approaching light at the end of a dark tunnel, shoring up his priceless faith. Although he had no idea what lay ahead, he saw just enough to know that one day all would be well. Nevertheless, throughout his years of confinement he must have been sorely tried and tested. Maybe there were doubts about his dreams. Were they really true? Maybe moments of despair when he thought he might never again see the light of day. Even worse were moments of isolation when he felt that he had been abandoned by God. Although such gruesome moments were an ordeal he weathered them.

The prison beneath Potiphar's mansion was manky, cramped and stuffy. Joseph, who had been immaculately turned out and groomed while working for Potiphar, soon found himself looking like any other prisoner. Human relations, he surely found, are much easier when food and water are readily available. It is easy to suffer long and be kind without the discomforts of a prison cell. It is far from easy to love our neighbour when those we are called to love are the lowest of the low. Joseph was patient throughout this testing time. When sorely tried he turned to prayer. Sometimes the best he could do was to cry out for help. Even when the climate in his cell was oppressive Joseph did his best to follow the royal pathway of love. Although the prisoners could see that Joseph was a man set apart, they didn't know what to make of him. His former status as the senior servant of Potiphar and the fact that he was a Hebrew slave did him no favours. He did his best not to be distracted by their envy of his peace and assurance or that he was called by God. In the pressure cooker of prison Joseph couldn't fail to realise that the tiniest spot of pride in his former status might put an end to his continuing journey of humble service. In the belly of the dungeon Joseph could clearly see that pride in his unique calling might yet prevent him from walking humbly with God and being content to do little things with great love.

*

To illustrate the snare of such a temptation, Olive Wyon told the story of Geoffrey Bull, a missionary in Tibet. After three years of fulfilling service, he was imprisoned and cruelly treated. His treasured Bible was taken away. He spent long periods meditating upon holy scripture. The opening of the door in Tibet had been replaced by the closed door of his cell. It was there that he began to ponder upon Abraham on Mount Moriah. *In my loneliness I followed Abraham all the way to the top of Mount Moriah. I watched him cutting wood and preparing fire. Can I follow the call of Abraham,* he wondered. What could he give up which was absolutely vital to him in that very moment. It was then that he realised that there was something to surrender which would cost him everything – his calling. God's call had become a career. The more he thought about it, the more he realised that even his vocation must be given up, for what God wanted wasn't even his missionary work in Tibet but himself. *While I had my call, in a way I had everything, so it too must go back to God who gave it.*

*

SURRENDER

After a tough schooling in the school of the Lord's service Joseph emerged from prison tempered like steel. The honeymoon period of prayer came to a sudden end in the pit. This was when his walk of faith and trust in divine providence really began. Having humbly dealt with his faults and failings in the presence of God, Joseph was prepared for changes in his way of prayer. Throughout a period of obscurity God was with him and in him. Joseph was especially thankful in these days that God provided human support from a sympathetic guard and the company of his cell mates, including the cup bearer to the Pharaoh and the baker. Moreover, because he held a supervisory role in the prison he was never at a loose end. In the doom-laden dungeon Joseph was a ray of light. There he learned that humility is sweeter than honey and that those who nourish themselves with this honey produce sweet fruit. Joseph had never been a rebellious teenager who couldn't wait to spread his wings. Although family life was far from perfect, he was happy enough at home working on the farm. As the years flew by Joseph found that homesickness gradually diminished as he became attuned to life in Egypt. Even in prison he found that he was free to love and to serve God. In moments of silence, his soul stilled in God's loving presence, he was to learn that it is God who interprets dreams. By surrendering himself to God he discovered God. It was in prison that Joseph learned the lesson of total surrender to divine providence and emerged a man brimming with self-confidence. As for his prayer, how can it be better expressed than in words from psalm 143:

O let me hear thy loving kindness in the morning, for in thee is my trust: show me the way that I should walk. Quicken me, O Lord, for thy name's sake; and for thy righteousness' sake bring my soul out of trouble.

While in captivity Joseph did his best to keep pride at bay so that he wasn't wrong-footed by self-righteousness. It was there he began to realise that paying attention to the care of the garden of the soul is a continuing work. Weeds, once dealt with, have a nasty habit of reappearing. Growing shrubs need support. Pests and aphids need to be removed. Gardens need watering. As he looked back Joseph could see that it was carelessness and complacency which had caused him to become ensnared by Potiphar's wife. In an inattentive moment they had been alone. In prison Joseph had plenty of time to ponder such things. There he learned that 'If I have faith, that can move mountains, but have not love I am nothing. If I give all my possessions to the poor and surrender my body to the flames but have not love, I gain nothing. Love is patient, love is kind. It does not envy, it does not boast, it is not proud. It is not rude, it is not self-seeking, it is not easily angered, it keeps no record of wrongs. Love does not delight in evil but rejoices with the truth. It always protects, always trusts, always hopes, always perseveres. Love never fails.' Finally, in the words of the St James Bible: 'Faith, hope and charity these three but the greatest of these is charity.'

By the time Joseph left prison he was prepared for the demanding years ahead. When released he overflowed with sacred love, not just for his family and friends but for all humanity, from the greatest to the least. In captivity he had learned to love his enemies and was content to serve as a slave in a foreign land. During his trials his heart became afflicted with pity for the poor, the downtrodden and the destitute – the more so because he himself had travelled on such a humiliating journey. In this schooling the renewal of his mind led to a deeper understanding of the love of God and what really made people tick. Little by little his heart began to burn with the fire of divine love as his soul became a living flame. People were drawn to him because he was charged with the magnetic power of divine love. Although the exhilarating experience of the love of God on the nursery slopes had long since faded, while stewing in prison he learned that 'the light shines in the darkness and the darkness has not overcome it.'

CHAPTER 4

Facing the Right Direction

In the early church the candidate turned West to renounce Satan and East to profess faith in the living risen Christ. William Law said that facing the wrong direction involved 'Not seeking everything we can to delight our senses, or by spending our time or money on pleasures, diversions, or worldly enjoyments while failing to exercise self-discipline and pray.' Day by day prayer is the lifeline which helps us to stay safely on course and to retain our focus on what God requires. While vicar of Braughing, I used to chat with Don McCullin, the photographer, at his garden gate close to the churchyard. One day he told me about the still photographs he had taken for the film *Blow-Up*. Evidence of the concealment of a murder was observed only after a photograph was blown up several times. It wasn't until then that it was possible to see an image no-one had previously noticed while looking at the long shot of the wider scene. Turning aside from the distractions of the world helps us to focus on every word that proceeds from the mouth of God. Focussing on all that God is doing and making known enables us to find our way along the journey of life. The Pharisee who went to the Temple to pray was blindsided by pride and hypocrisy. The publican was not. Turning around and sharpening our focus helps us to see more clearly, love more dearly, and follow our Lord more nearly day by day.

*

THE FRUITFUL PRAYER OF JOSEPH

That Joseph became a living prayer is evidenced by the man he became. No doubt his prayer was straightforward. He talked to God. He listened to God. He thought about God and spent time in silent loving attention, like Mary of Bethany at Jesus' feet. During heart-to-heart exchanges with God, Joseph identified and rooted out lingering traces of pride. Clothed in the love and mercy of God he saw for himself its corrosive effects. He also saw that there was more to repentance than apologising through gritted teeth or issuing a prepared statement. Neither did he fall into the trap of false humility by owning up to responsibility for sins he didn't commit. He wasn't to blame for the sins of his father or grandfather, let alone the sin of Cain. Nor did he go around sheepishly saying that he was a worm and no man and an outcast of the people. Rather he quietly rejoiced at the liberating blessing of sin forgiven. When pride tried to distract him, by stoking up regrets about past years or fears for the future, he did his best to stay focussed. Moreover, as he grew in humility he began to see that impurities such as a flash of anger, a moment of impatience, a half-truth, a sinful thought, envy, fear, doubt and the sins of the flesh, waved aside as of little consequence in his youth, had spawned unintended consequences. By unburdening his soul in prayer, he was able to travel light. Moreover, he found that when God addressed his sin it was always in love. When God made known his imperfections, he became ever more aware that the God of love was with him and in him.

*

LIVING PRAYER

By facing God, we are schooled in the way to do all that we do graciously, compassionately, carefully, thoroughly, attentively and honestly. While facing God our lives are enlightened by sacred love. A desire for such love is deeply rooted at the core of every human heart. The wellspring of such love is a heart centred on God. Daily prayer lays the foundations. Becoming a living prayer is a lifetime choice. It isn't easy. We may not feel like it. We don't know what to say. We set aside time and the minute hand on the clock never moves. Tired, we fall asleep. Disturbed by the doorbell or a ping from an iPhone we are distracted. Sometimes we are busy. At others we don't feel like praying. Nevertheless, even when run off our feet there are opportunities to say a simple prayer. Waking or sleeping we are never alone. Moreover, be assured that the desire to pray is itself a prayer. A single dart of longing love pierces the cloud of unknowing. Moreover, although the natural gift for prayer is heaven sent it requires perseverance. Further, if we wish to alter our lives we must alter our hearts. It is impossible to live one way and to pray another. Prayer is the work of a hospitable heart. A heart which desires to keep the two great commands. Without prayer our hearts atrophy as we give way to anxious fears, wants, desires, ambitions or covetousness. Further, in spite of our best efforts, pride will always be at the door trying to trip us up and to prevent us loving our brother whom we have seen and our neighbour as our self. Blindness to the machinations of pride might well be caused because we are looking the wrong way. God, in his love, mercy, care and sensitivity, makes such truth known in his own good time. As we stumble in the dark, we learn hard lessons from bumping into things we cannot see. Further, if we are wholly preoccupied with our own affairs, our own wellbeing, or spiritual state we will soon fail to notice God's sealed orders. Should we be preoccupied with the treasures of the material world we might never set out in pursuit of the pearl of great price. Be sober, be vigilant, for even little things may trip us up. As Francis de Sales said, it doesn't matter if a bird is held by a rope or a thread – it still cannot fly.

LISTENING

Living prayer involves constantly paying attention to God in matters both great and small. Timing is everything. Prayer is always answered in God's way. Sometimes in short order. For example, one day I was warned by a woman who had just driven into the village that I would never get into Peterhead because of a traffic jam. The stationary queue, I was informed, was more than a mile long. My first anxious thought was to ring up and cancel an important appointment. Before doing this, I paused for a moment of silence. It was quite clear. *Go to the top of the hill and see if things are moving.* It seemed to me to be of the spirit. Even though spiritual things are discerned spiritually it is good to consider them carefully. There were three confirmations. There was no good reason why I might not do this. It wasn't in conflict with more important responsibilities. As it would only take two or three minutes to get to the top of the hill it wouldn't even delay cancellation of the appointment. At the top of the hill at a T junction the line of traffic was just beginning to crawl, and someone immediately let me in. Once on the main road, the traffic began to move, and I was just in time for my appointment. On the other hand, my requests for my twin brother to be spared from serious mental illness were answered in a very different way. When I found him sitting like a stone statue, catatonic, and bloated with insulin after weeks in a psychiatric hospital, I was helpless. As I consider this, I recall the words of St Paul. Three times I besought the Lord about this. And the response, *My grace is sufficient for you.* The answer to prayer was the provision of grace to cope with a difficult situation. For half a century God's grace was sufficient as we saw little things worked together for good, not least when, two decades later, he settled down happily with his partner and resumed his painting. But in his mortal life he never fully recovered. He remained on anti-psychotic medication for the rest of his days. As I sat on my twin's bed shortly

27

before he died and showed him photographs of his art exhibition in Aberdeen, I thanked God that He had always loved my twin with his immeasurable love. This precious moment will stay with me for the rest of my life. Just before Christmas, a festival on which he had often been so alone and isolated as many families turned in on themselves, he died at peace in the middle of the night.

*

LIGHT AT THE END OF THE TUNNEL

While in prison Joseph made good use of his time. He stood toe to toe with pride, humbly supported his cellmates, interpreted their dreams. and assisted the prison keeper as he continued his walk with God. Such service issued from a stilled soul. Moreover, Joseph was aware that God knew what he needed before he asked and only gives good gifts to his children. He also realised that the reason for making his requests known unto God wasn't to change God's mind but to fall in line with what he is doing. He learned that the light of God's love is unapproachable. Even the tiniest reflection of that love darkens our eyes so that we cannot see. It is a darkness in which we may walk hand in hand with God. It is a darkness in which things are made known. It is a darkness in which we feel deserted but are enfolded in God's love. Such darkness isn't to be confused with darkness caused by indifference or serious sin. It isn't the mist and haze which obscures our view when we wander from the pathway. In this darkness we may not see the distant scene but learn to be content to take the next little step. For this darkness isn't the darkness of despair or the lethargy of sickness. After being out in bright sunlight, it is dark when we go in. We can hardly see until our eyes adjust. After a glimpse of the light of God it is dark. When we go in, we see just enough to find our way around a familiar space and so are equipped to focus on what God is doing and what is required of us. The fruit of the prayer of Joseph is to be seen in his focus on God and his close observance of the second great command by caring for his own family, his companions in prison, and the poor of the land. Daily Joseph will have thanked God for meeting his immediate needs and counted his blessings. His deeply rooted love of God ensured that nothing could rob him of his joy. Nevertheless, there must have been days when far from finding prayer easy it was hard going. The man he became suggests that years spent in exile and confinement purged his soul. Even in his darkest night he never lost sight of the glimmer of light at the end of the tunnel. So it was that Joseph emerged from his trials the confident but humble man who was escorted to Pharaoh.

TRAVELLING LIGHT

Those travelling light on the journey of prayer experience deep peace. It is only withheld as a reminder of what it is like to walk alone. Francis de Sales illustrated such a moment in his account of a night when he lay awake all night, anxious about a small matter. He contrasted this with the peace he experienced when his life was in danger on his mission to the Chablais. Joseph was able to travel light because, like the humble page who walked in the footmarks of the good king, he had no luggage. Travelling light Joseph found himself at the right place at the right time to interpret the dreams of Pharaoh. By then he could review the painful memories of the last thirteen years in a wholly new way. He could look back at the cruel landscape through the window of charity. His intimacy with God opened his eyes to a distant scene which no longer rankled but was bathed in the light of the merciful love of God. Freed from the sickening memories of the past Joseph was free to move on. That he finally reached such a place is to be seen in the way he was so comfortable with his Egyptian captors and conducted himself in prison.

*

Providence is the guidance of the Holy Spirit working all things together for good. My first curacy was in a busy town parish. It was a twenty-four-seven existence and I was still pursuing academic interests as well as having weighty family responsibilities. One day I was driving home when I saw all the houses by the roadside caving in. I was exhausted and felt that I had lost my bearings. It was while reading the *Church Times* that I saw an advertisement for a curate in a group of country parishes in North-east Wiltshire. This I saw to be the next step. So I answered the advertisement. My wife and I drove down to meet the rector and to see the parishes. As I knelt before the altar in a delightful little parish church in the tiny village of Slaughterford I knew that this was where God was calling us to be. It was earthed. I well recall a service at that church in which the number of people present to give thanks for the harvest was greater than the number living in the village. It turned out to be a place for recovery after several demanding years. I didn't then know that Biddestone Rectory, the Victorian rectory where we were to live, accessed by a drive some two hundred and fifty yards long lined with lime trees and carpeted with snow drops in the new year, was to become a refuge for my parents and grandmother after a crisis, following which they had to move house and join us. Almost three years later, after a period of rural convalescence, I was ready to move on so once again responded to an advertisement in the *Church Times* and was appointed vicar of the hidden village of Braughing in Hertfordshire.

CHAPTER 5

God Speaks To Us Today

God communicates in myriads of ways. He communicates through our human nature, through instinct, intuition and intelligence. He speaks to us through our conscience. He speaks through other people and events. He speaks through dreams and visions or sends messengers to help us or to redirect us when we are lost. Above all he speaks to us through the living word, the truth of God incarnate who illuminates the inner chambers of the soul. When I was young dreams and visions were often considered to be either nonsense, of no consequence, or determined by eating cheese before we went to bed. Our evaluation of dreams therefore might well be clouded by the spirit of the age. Cynics dismiss them. The credulous are easily deceived. To benefit from the content of dreams it is important to employ intelligence to evaluate them along with intuitive and prayerful assessments of their meaning and purpose. Many dreams address our personal situation. Some have wider implications. In the Bible we see the importance of significant dreams which have far-reaching consequences. Such were the dreams of Joseph. So too those of his father Jacob, who laid his head on a pillow of stone and dreamt that there was a ladder from earth to heaven with angels ascending and descending. Then the promise. 'Behold I am with you and will bring you back to this promised land.' Even Pilate's wife figures because her dream during a troubled night before the trial of Jesus caused her to warn Pontius Pilate about the events of the coming day. St Paul was directed to introduce the Gospel to Europe in a dream about a man of Macedonia bidding him welcome, so changed his itinerary. When I was young dreams were too readily reduced to being purely imagination. Freud paved the way for a fresh understanding of dreams. Jung understood them to be important evidence to be closely examined even if difficult to interpret or contrary to preconceived ideas. Dreams are important bearers of truth. Jacob acknowledged the importance of what he had seen when he said, 'Surely the Lord is in this place and I did not know it.' In his darkest hours the dreams of Joseph helped him to see that it wasn't blind fate which caused him to be thrown down a pit or locked up in prison but divine providence preparing him for his mission in Egypt.

*

IF YOU ARE FAITHFUL

A group was standing in a circle after a service at which Jean Darnall had been the speaker, when she was caught up in the spirit and uttered a prophetic word. It began with words about a man being here who had a costly ministry and continued with words about the need for faithfulness in prayer. When I asked about its meaning, she simply said, 'It was for you.' It is over forty years ago now, but I can still recall the urgency of her words as she spoke about the need for faithful prayer. Of its importance there was no doubt. I recall her saying, 'If you are faithful, if you are faithful,' followed by the words 'the best is yet to come.' A year or two later she came to speak in St John's Church, Digswell. As we walked back to the rectory she saw Digswell House, then an arts centre, looking sad and uncared for and in need of renovation. She turned on her heel to have a good look and after a moment's silence said, 'The Lord wants that house.'

In 1988 a dream had profound consequences for St John's Church. In a little book published in 2012 Susan Richardson wrote:

I woke up with a certain sense of urgency. Had I overslept? I looked at the clock; it was 3.05a.m. I certainly hadn't overslept so why had I awakened with such a start? I turned over and tried to go to sleep, but to no avail. A word, a thought, an idea, call it what you will, crept into my mind. *Get up and pray about the church finances.* Madness, I thought. I didn't know anything about the church finances and had no desire to know anything about them and anyway it was the middle of the night! I put my head under the duvet and tried to go back to sleep. The niggling sense of the need to get up and pray would not go away. After tossing and turning for a while I eventually got up. It was now 3.45 a.m. I was certainly not feeling remotely holy or reverential – in fact I was decidedly grumpy. I would need to be up in less than three hours to get the family up and out. As I stumbled about the kitchen the cats looked at me with a mixture of curiosity and caution. Having made some tea I sat down and pointed out to God what a crazy idea this was, mumbled something about blessings for the church and suggested it would be more sensible in future to wake up somebody who knew about these matters. After sitting for a little while another word, thought, or whatever, crept into my mind. *Turn, turn back to me in prayer and all will be well.* I went back to bed, perplexed, and decided to try to forget all about it. I went back to sleep quite quickly and then had the following dream. A church collection plate is piled high with notes. On top is a cheque from the Bradford and Bingley Building society for £500.

She shared this dream with a friend, who told her that her church, St John's Digswell, was in need of further funds and that she should come to see me. This was followed by an extraordinary response; the enrichment of the ministry of St John's Church throughout the following decade, the launch of the ministry in Digswell House, in the house we called St James House, the planting of the Rose of Sharon society, all underpinned by a response to the call to prayer. At the time of her dream Susan Richardson didn't attend St John's Church but came to see me and shared what she had seen. I invited her to the Church finance committee where she shared the words, *Turn back to me in prayer and all will be well.* On the Sunday that we invited people to respond to the vision for the church the collection plate was piled high with notes – ten times the amount presented on the same Sunday the previous year. On top was a cheque for £500 drawn on the Bradford and Bingley Building society. Thus was our attention called to the need for a return to prayer. For several years when uncertain about where to go I had had dreams about being lost while driving through familiar streets. There was no need for an interpreter. My impatience was the problem. On the other hand, the dreams of Joseph had far-reaching implications. They were the kind of dreams you never forget. Joseph kept them close. They were his ray of hope. My father had a reassuring personal dream reported in a carefully preserved letter to his sister, Sister Edith OHP, which was passed to me after she died. In this dream my father saw the sad, bare room where my grandfather lay dying, a sick and unhappy man, a decade after he had suffered a serious stroke. Photographs I retain of the bareness of that house reveal the sparse furnishings, brown furniture, wooden chairs and bare floors. During the dream he saw his father being raised up. The room was filled with light and his father radiant and at peace. When my grandfather died in 1941 in England my father was serving with the Royal Engineers in charge of all the military properties in Iceland.

*

THE MINISTRY OF JOSEPH

The cupbearer and the baker shared their dreams with Joseph. They were troubled and confused. Joseph discerned them spiritually so to the cupbearer he said, 'In three days Pharaoh will lift up your head and restore you to your office,' and to the baker, 'In three days Pharaoh will lift up your head from you and you will be hanged on a tree.' Before he was released Joseph asked the cupbearer to remember him. It is said that the cupbearer forgot. Perhaps he was simply waiting for a propitious moment. When it suited he remembered! During the two years of continuing incarceration Joseph never lost sight of the glimmer of light at the end of the tunnel. Wherever he was called to be and whatever he was called to do Joseph had learned that the grace of God is more than sufficient. Sometimes he was aware of what God required and gladly seconded his proposals. At others he simply found himself about God's business doing little things with great love. Meanwhile he carried on with his work in the prison after getting up, saying his prayers, and doing whatever he had to do while keeping alert in order to make sure that he was always attentive to sealed orders. For two long years the cupbearer was silent. Although an important person he was in awe of Pharaoh so waited and waited for a moment to speak to him about Joseph. Such a moment never came until he saw Pharaoh in a two and eight about his dreams, waving his arms around in frustration and booting out his magicians and wise men when they were unable to interpret them When the cupbearer saw the hullabaloo he thought that when things had settled down there might be a chance to speak to Pharaoh about Joseph. Maybe he hoped that, once Pharaoh's dreams were interpreted, he would find himself in his good books and be rewarded. So having smartened up he approached Pharaoh with due deference and braced himself to tell him all about the young Hebrew in prison who could interpret dreams. In no time at all bathed, shaved and decently attired Joseph was brought before Pharaoh. Joseph humbly explained to him that it was God rather than Joseph who was the interpreter of dreams. Only after Joseph had explained where he was coming from did Pharaoh tell him all about his two confusing dreams.

The first dream was deeply disturbing. It concerned seven fat and seven thin cows. The fat cows were gross and the thin emaciated. There followed a ghastly scene in which the emaciated cows gobbled up the fat ones. Deeply troubled, Pharaoh said that he had fallen asleep again and had a second dream. In this dream seven ears of corn, plump and healthy, were eaten up by seven ears of blighted corn. After reminding Pharaoh that God is the interpreter of dreams Joseph explained that seven years of plenty would be followed by seven years of famine.

*

While writing this book I have been thinking about the night in 1945 when I was directed to the story of Joseph. It must have been a vivid dream. Eighty years later I can see the place I was standing in the hall of Woodhouse Manor farm when my mother and grandmother helped me to put on my brand-new coat. It was a close woven tweed in blues, greens and browns, made from a pre-war quality tweed jacket. Compared with Jacob's gift of the coat of many colours to Joseph mine was a humble garment. Nevertheless, it was very special in a period of clothes rationing when all our clothes for more than a decade were hand-me-downs. It mattered not that the sleeves were too long and kept my hands warm. It was my own dream coat, and I was very proud! The dream followed the panoramic view of my life in which I saw or heard nothing but simply knew that God would lead me on. There would be setbacks. I would be called to travel light and was aware that I was called to rely on divine providence. It has been said that on life's journey the time might well come when we find ourselves as if at an airport, checking in to travel to a new destination. No luggage, we learn, might be taken on this flight. It is time to downsize. Not just the clutter but things that we have treasured all our lives must be left behind before we can board the little plane for the next leg of our solo journey. Doubt will urge us to draw back and remain with cherished belongings. It is only when we realise that it isn't possible to die to self unless prepared to relinquish our grasp on all such attachments that we are free to move. Only when I let go of my ministry and tried to focus on God's proposals did the way ahead open up. So it was that all the resources were provided for acquiring St James House and running it for the seven years which had been indicated from day one. When it closed, the call was to withdraw for prayer and intercession. For this purpose we were called to find a hotel. After a long search, the ruins of the Earl's Lodge hotel were located in Boddam in north-east Scotland. This was acquired for retirement for prayer. Seven years after St James House was closed the ruined hotel had been successfully converted into Buchanness Lodge – a hotel acquired for the hospitality of intercession. This was the fulfilment of the second part of my dream as a child which I was too young to understand, the call to prayer. Over many years I learned that if God wills the end, he also wills the means. St Theresa of Lisieux learned this simple lesson when relinquishing her ambitions to be a teacher and missionary and was content to stay in her sick room responding to the call to love her carers. This was when she cried out, 'At last I have found my vocation. My vocation is to love.' Once Joseph had been thoroughly purged in the refiner's fire he emerged ablaze with the love of God. In spite of his tribulations, he too had learned that if God wills the end, he also wills the means, and was content to place his trust in divine providence. So he emerged from prison a chastened, holy man whose delight was to watch and to wait, to love and serve.

CHAPTER 6

The Work of God

When I was about to study economics, the first line in the set book I was supposed to read said that profit is the end of economic man. I never read the next line. It seemed to me to bear no relationship with either household management or to what really matters to ordinary people. I can't remember now if I failed the exam or never turned up! The value of work doesn't depend simply on its execution or profitability but the spirit in which it is done. The Good Samaritan did more than saying are you alright, help the victim to stand up, and give him a couple of coins. He did more than bathe his wounds beside the rough-hewn bumpy road from Jerusalem to Jericho. Having done all he could, he made arrangements for him to be cared for. The idea that work is solely paid employment and that those who either cannot or are not called to work contribute nothing is blinkered. So too the foolish notion that while not engaged in paid employment the rest of our lives are worthless and of no consequence. Such an approach devalues the contribution of the elderly, the house-bound, the handicapped, the mentally ill and many others who for whatever reason are unable to find or incapable of employment. Sole focus on profit devalues the work of stay-at-home wives, mothers and children. It overlooks the priceless contribution of grandparents to our society. It devalues the contribution of the handicapped. It ignores the contribution of the elderly monk who realised that he could do more good sitting in his chair at prayer in his final days than he had in the whole of his active life as a missionary and teacher. The work of God involves being constantly alert ready to love, and serve whether at home, work, rest or play. It doesn't involve pulling down our barns and building greater to fill our coffers so that we might become comfortable couch potatoes in slippers, so attached to our worldly goods that, like Mr Scrooge, we will never part with a penny. In other words, work is doing God's thing not our own. This is what Jesus was saying to his parents when he explained why he lingered in the Temple in discussions with the elders when he was a boy. He was doing the work he was called to do. He was about his Father's business. This involves doing the things we have to do because we are who we are, and we are where we are. The labours of Joseph were extensive. He worked on the home farm. He served God in prison. He administered the distribution of corn in Egypt. He was also a dutiful son, a faithful husband, and a good father. Above all he walked with God so all that he did was undergirded by prayer.

Until the sixteenth century work was primarily home-based subsistence living. As I looked back at generations of my Cloke forbears, which go back as far as 1520, I saw that they remained in Southern Kent for five hundred years. When Henry Cloke married Joan unknown there is no mention of their employment. From the eighteenth century, occupations begin to appear. So Benjamin Cloke, born in 1734 in Stowing in Kent, is described as a farm labourer. Rosetta Cloke, born in 1847 in Canterbury, was a milliner, dressmaker. William Allchin, born in 1800, was a carpenter and builder. Fanny Allchin, my great-great-grand-mother, was a school mistress and so on. Moreover, people weren't necessarily doing a single job. Henry Spencer Cloke, born in 1835, was a plumber, glazier and victualler. By the end of the nineteenth century, we find Clokes entering the professions such as schoolteacher, architect and bank manager. These family records trace the long journey from the time when work was primarily home-based, tilling the soil, and cottage industries creeping step by step to the model more familiar today. Nowadays the daily round and trivial task still include home and family responsibilities, shopping, cooking, putting out the bins, and loving our neighbour. The work required of us includes things which simply crop up. Matthew 25 highlights natural duties which have nothing to do with paid employment: for example, the call to feed the hungry, visit the sick and those in prison, or to stop to offer support whenever we can. One dark evening I saw a tiny flicker of light as I drove down a Wiltshire country road. It was no more than a pin prick issuing from a fountain pen torch with a failing battery. As I drove past, I just noticed it and wondered what it was. I turned the car round to have a look. When I got out, I looked down the steep slope on the sharp bend and saw a car lying some way down on its side. It was invisible from the road. Two young women on the way to sing in a concert in Bath were signalling with their fountain pen torch. We took them to the Rectory to warm up and made sure they reached their destination on time. Loving service is its own reward. It is good to treasure such moments but all too easy to miss opportunities to respond to God's call to respond to those in need.

Recently I read that voluntary work in the UK was valued at more than the GDP of our country. I was hardly surprised. St James House today would cost £1,000,000. Apart from myself as Rector no-one was paid. There were no grants. There were no fund-raising activities. Had we paid those who were on duty from 9am to 9pm seven days a week at a carer's pay today, the cost would have amounted to another £1,000,000. The additional contribution of teachers, social workers, nurses and other volunteers who freely gave their support is incalculable. But the real value of what took place cannot be measured in this way. Quite simply, for many visitors and helpers it was life-changing. It was the loving service which made it so. Work isn't earning money but loving service. 'This is the work of God that you believe in the one whom he has sent' (John 6 29). This includes the cultivation through prayer and Godly living of the gifts and graces which enrich every moment of every day and a willingness to step out in faith. One day a locution took me by surprise. *I want you to be a fool for my sake!* This came as a reminder that my work was not mine but his. My call was to work with God rather than trying to keep everyone happy. This changed everything. Much of the work wasn't so different but there was a willingness to be content, to see no further than the next step. Moreover, it was not just the work itself which mattered but the motivation for doing it and the spirit in which it was done. Prayer enables us to focus on what to do and when to leave well alone. From day one we were made aware St James House would continue for just seven years.

*

THE RENEWED JOSEPH

While in captivity Joseph learned that humility involves being a fool for the sake of God. The humbled prisoner was surprisingly confident in Pharaoh's presence and boldly advised Pharaoh that there was an immediate need for a vizier. Humility enabled him calmly to accept the post. As vizier he was called to serve as minister of supplies for the whole of Egypt. Such a demanding post required adjustments to his life of prayer. While in solitude he will have learned that prayer is a heart-to-heart exchange with God. In his demanding role as vizier Joseph will have discovered a new way of praying while working all hours. He will have paid closer attention to what God required throughout the day. In this way he was to become a praying presence while working his socks off to ensure that no-one would starve. His radiant humanity was evidence of his intimacy with God, so too the sight of him humbly mingling with the poorest in the land. Prayer for Joseph had always been natural. The home base of his prayer might have been like those of Daniel who made space for prayer three times a day. Faced with a well-nigh impossible task, Joseph learned to pray without ceasing. As well as constantly mulling things over with God, at times he was lost in wonder, love, and praise. As a child he had learned to still his soul in such a way that he wasn't disturbed by the familiar sounds of life on the farm. So when the famine began, he wasn't distracted by the noise of the crowds in the market place. Such music framed the silence – a silence charged with an awareness of the love of God. Even while in prison Joseph had constantly found a way to be still and sink down beneath his troubled thoughts to commune with his heavenly Father. This prepared him for what lay ahead.

*

SACRED SILENCE

A beautiful young woman in the melee of a very active social life, who was due to marry an eligible young man within the week, suddenly saw during a Minuet a vision of the world dying for lack of prayer. She could almost hear the world gasping as a drowning man gasps for air. The dance now seemed Macabre. In the corner was a priest, discussing a suitable marriage for a young woman with her mother. Even the church, the dancer realised, did not see that the world was dying for lack of prayer. As instantly as a leaping flame she vowed her life to ceaseless intercession. She turned on her heel and left everything behind, to found a contemplative community. During the never-ending days of early childhood, in the solitude and silence of a hill farm, my life was accompanied by the lowing of the cattle, the music of running water, and an occasional air raid siren. Long periods of silence were interrupted by cockcrow, squealing pigs, and the occasional sound of the tractor setting off for the fields. It was a different world. One day Phillip, a young man of about eighteen, dressed in plus fours like a companion of Bertie Wooster, walked into the yard to help with the haymaking. On another a transient Irish labourer was to be found sleeping in bales of hay in the shippon because he was too flea-ridden to enter the house. But all along there was silence and more silence. No longer driven by the need to study or disturbed by lorries pulling up outside my bedroom window in Gower Street at 5am on the way to Covent Garden, I rediscovered the loving attention I had known as a child. On leaving a silent retreat at St Katherine's, Stepney, I was reluctant to speak. By the time I got home I realised that such moments are gifts of God to be cherished but relinquished as soon the moment has passed. In an active and demanding life, it is easier to make space for moments of prayer during routine tasks than many suppose. A heart-to-heart exchange with God is possible in undemanding occupations such as housework, driving to work, walking to the letter box, taking a bath or shower, Zooming, on the phone, or even while writing a book! The deepest prayer is attentive silence. The more active we become the more we need to seize moments for prayer. Living prayer issues from longings and aspirations and bears fruit in words and deeds. When we find adequate space for prayer, we become more aware of the hand of divine providence during the coming day.

THY WILL BE DONE

The Lord's prayer is brief and to the point. We are called to love and worship our heavenly Father as we pray thy kingdom come. The words 'Thy will be done' remind us of Mary's fiat 'Let it be unto me according to thy word.' Give us this day our daily bread recalls that all we need God hath provided. The bread of life is food for tomorrow as well as today – the bread of heaven That we might know the deeps of God's mercy we forgive others so that we might know the fullness of the joy of sin forgiven. Finally, a petition that we might be delivered from the claws of the evil one. According to Metropolitan Anthony, doing the will of God involves:

Doing it in every detail, at every moment, to the utmost of our power, as perfectly as we can, with the greatest moral integrity, using our intelligence, our imagination, our will, our skill, our experience, so that we can gradually learn to be strictly, earnestly obedient to our Lord.

Unless we do this, our discipleship is a set of self-imposed rules which make us self-satisfied, leaves us nowhere, because the essential momentum of our discipleship is to allow the Lord Christ to be our mind, our will and our heart. Unless we renounce ourselves and accept his life in place of our life, unless we aim at what St Paul defines as 'It is no longer I but Christ who lives in me', we shall never either be disciplined or a disciple. Let us rise in the morning and offer ourselves to God. We have woken from a sleep which divides us from yesterday. Waking up offers us a new reality, a day which has never existed before, an unknown time and space stretching before us like a field of untrodden snow. Let us ask the Lord to bless this day and bless us in it. On the cross on Good Friday Jesus Christ looked upon the crowds saying, 'Father, forgive them for they know not what they do.' There was no impassioned speech, no support for freedom fighters who wanted to overthrow the might of Rome. Self-offering was his resistance.

THE CHANGE IN JOSEPH

We know little about the prayer of Joseph but see the fruit of his intimacy with God. Joseph surely learned that it is only when our lives are based on humble prayer and self-offering that our work will truly be God's work. Then it will be neither laced with an egotistical desire to feel good about our self, beguiled by the world's faint praise, or deceived by the mirage of our dearest idols. It is in prayer that we are equipped for God's work. Prayer is the bedrock of Godly living. Being attentive to what God is doing facilitates God's work. It is in heart-to-heart prayer that we learn to unreservedly pray, 'Thy kingdom come, thy will be done.'

CHAPTER 7

The Reunion

CORN IN EGYPT

A fflicted by gnawing hunger when the Egyptian famine raged as far afield as Hebron, Joseph's brothers made their way to Egypt for supplies of corn. They were immediately impressed by the slick distribution, marvelling at the vizier in fine robes. Everything was being done decently and in good order. Moreover, the vizier was talking to every individual as if each one was special. His brothers didn't realise that the vizier was their lost brother Joseph. No longer a young man, Joseph was dressed in posh Egyptian clothing and spoke their language fluently. When his brothers came before him with their sacks he spoke brusquely to them. Disguising his voice, he asked if they had any other brothers. It was because he was using an interpreter that his brothers continued talking to one another, not realising that he understood their asides. Joseph was pleased to see signs of change. They were less surly, more courteous and surprisingly at ease while speaking freely and answering his questions. So when asked if they had a younger brother they didn't hesitate to tell him about Benjamin, who had stayed at home with their father Jacob. For over a decade Joseph had prayed that his family might one day be reconciled. Nevertheless, before he made himself known he needed to be sure that it would be safe to entrust them with the care of Benjamin and their father. Before they went home with their sacks jam packed with corn, they were ordered not to return for further supplies without bringing Benjamin with them. This rattled the brothers. They deeply regretted mentioning Benjamin because they knew that Jacob would never let him go. On their way home they hadn't gone far when they found the money they had paid for the corn in their sacks and panicked. They travelled as fast as they could, worried that if they were caught, they might be tied up and sold as slaves. Relieved to be back home on the farm they told Jacob about their adventures and the vizier who commanded them to bring Benjamin with them on their return. Jacob was distressed that they had so much as mentioned Benjamin. As the seasons flew by the famine raged. Because of the money found in their sacks and the command to take Benjamin with them, none of the family wanted to go back to Egypt in spite of the fact that Simeon was held hostage. For a while life on the farm carried on as before. As the famine grew worse and worse the bleached landscape became littered with the bones and rotting carcases of dead animals surrounded by circling birds of prey. As Jacob looked out across the fields, he realised that there was really no alternative but to go back to Egypt for more corn. And yet he hesitated because he was worried that if Benjamin went back to Egypt with his brothers he might never come back. Still mourning the death of his beloved Rachel and the loss of Joseph, the thought of losing Benjamin increased his misery. He delayed as long as he could before finally giving his paternal blessing, saying, 'May almighty God grant you mercy before the man, and may he send back your other brother. And as for me I am bereaved of my children.' In order to reassure Jacob, Reuben offered to slay two of his own sons if they didn't bring Benjamin home.

The journey to Egypt is summed up in a sentence. 'So they took Benjamin and double the money and stood before the man.' Because of the money found in their sacks the brothers were jittery as they stood before the vizier. They were even more nervous when led to his house. The very idea that they might be forced into slavery gave them the collywobbles. So they got into a huddle and prepared an apology. When the opportunity arose, they said to the vizier, 'My Lord, we came down to buy food. When we came to a lodging place, we opened our sacks and behold there was money in each man's sack, our money. We have brought it back, together with other money to buy more food. We have no idea how it got there.' The long delay in the return of his brothers to collect further supplies troubled Joseph. It had been so long since they went home that he had begun to wonder if they would ever return. The brothers, however, were surprised by the warmth of his words. 'Peace be to you. Don't be afraid. Your God and the God of your father has put treasure in your sacks for you. I received your money.'

They were then asked, 'How are things back home?'

Overwhelmed by such a friendly welcome his brothers all bowed their heads and prostrated themselves on the ground before him. Joseph was completely undone. So his dreams were true. His brothers had just bowed down to him exactly as they had in his dream. As he gazed at Benjamin, now grown up, he could see the little child full of joy and laughter running around amongst the stoops of corn. Deeply moved, Joseph hurried out to find a place to weep. He wept because he saw signs of change in his brothers. He wept because Jacob had let Benjamin go. He wept because at last they were all together again. In order to celebrate, he invited his brothers to a feast. As vizier he dined on his own because of his rank. Because of their race the brothers also dined alone. At the feast a steward was instructed to make sure that the brothers were plied with good food and drink and had special instructions to make sure there was lashings of food and drink for Benjamin.

THE SILVER CUP

In order to further test their loyalty orders were again given for their money to be put back in their sacks. It is hard to know exactly what was in Joseph's mind, but he clearly wanted to find out if they could be trusted. It was wisdom that took such precautions, not a desire to ruffle their feathers. As well as the money hidden in the sacks his own priceless silver cup was placed in Benjamin's sack. Adorned with precious stones it was something every Egyptian nobleman might have owned. It might have been a present. Maybe it was a gift from Pharaoh. Maybe it was a wedding gift from Potiphera, his father-in-law. He was high priest of the Sun God in On and head of the most learned sacerdotal college in the country. A man of high rank. The silver cup was treasured because it was an acknowledgement of Joseph's status and position amongst the Egyptian elite. It was a priceless drinking cup as well as the cup filled with water that he used while prayerfully trying to discern the will of God. Maybe the cup was put in Benjamin's sack as an act of self-denial as he responded to a call for a closer walk with God. The brothers hadn't gone far on their way home when Joseph's steward caught up with them. A quick search unearthed the payment money in all their sacks and the silver cup in Benjamin's. Immediately they were charged with theft. This was the moment when Joseph's brothers faced up to their sin. Their confession concerned not only the cup and the money but their past failings for they said, 'God has found out the guilt of your servants, both we and the man also in whose hand the cup has been found.'

Although Joseph realised that his brothers seemed to have no intention of abandoning Benjamin, he wanted to make sure. So the brothers were told to go back home but that Benjamin would be kept on as a slave. Judah, the brother who came up with the idea of selling Joseph into slavery, volunteered to take Benjamin's place by offering to remain in Egypt as a servant. This was further reassurance that his brothers had no intention of ditching Benjamin. Confident now that his brothers had sufficiently changed their ways, Joseph felt it was the moment to tell them who he really was.

'Come close to me,' he said, 'I am your brother Joseph, the one you sold into Egypt.' On seeing their amazement Joseph continued, 'And now don't be angry at yourselves because you sold me here, for God sent me here before you to preserve life. He sent me ahead of you to preserve for you a remnant on earth, and to save your lives by a great deliverance.'

When Pharaoh heard the good news about this reunion, he issued a warm invitation, 'Load your animals and return to the land of Canaan and bring your father and your families to me. I will give you the best of the land of Egypt.'

The love which blossomed in the heart of Joseph after he left home was exponentially enriched. The more receptive he became to the love of God the greater love's increase. Exile was the theatre of God's love in which his soul matured. The fine wine of forgiveness and mercy not only set his brothers free but paved the way for their lives in Goshen. In the years to come after severe trials and testing in the wilderness the brothers of Joseph were to become patriarchs of the twelve tribes of Israel. As soon as his family arrived in Egypt, however, Joseph searched high and low for the best place to settle. After a thorough search he discovered the land of Goshen in the north-east of Egypt, not far from the Nile delta. It was a fertile land – an ideal place for his family to settle. With his well-known diplomatic skill he persuaded Pharaoh that it would be good to award this land to the seventy members of his Hebrew family. So it was that the land of Goshen became a precious gift from the Pharaoh himself.

*

TRUTH AND RECONCILIATION

When I was a child, I was given a children's Bible. It had the inviting aroma of a brand-new glossy book cover. It was a birthday present given to me in Woodhouse Manor farm. I remember kneeling at my grandmother's pink nursing chair, placing the book on the seat and kneeling down, captivated by the illustrations. It was probably from this treasured gift that the story of Joseph was first read to me. Love, mercy, forgiveness and reconciliation were at the core of his ministry. So too that of Desmond Tutu. While a student I remember talking to him about his interest in the Old Testament prophets, not realising that this same man was to be a servant leader who was to exercise a prophetic ministry in South Africa. In the senate house while waiting in a side room for a viva, we sat and looked at one another nervously across the room. He looked very different while courageously facing down the crowds in Soweto. Since he died, I have often thought about his life story. In the 1960s I lunched with Trevor Huddlestone in London, who probably had no idea of the spark he lit when he raised his hat to a black woman and visited her sickly child Desmond in hospital. The child became the schoolmaster. The schoolmaster became the priest, the priest became a bishop and the bishop became an arch-bishop. When I saw him on television, facing up to necklacing crowds, I could hardly believe my eyes. There he was, a fragile, good-natured man, charged with the love of God, standing up to evil with good in a bid to set his people free. He wasn't a Goliath. He was a Godly man who commanded the crowds not by might but by the Spirit of God. He bore witness to a central truth in the Gospel. The love of power leads to all manner of ills. The power of love is a healing and restorative gift of God. For the love of God is pure and undefiled, holy and enduring. It is that perfect love which animates and enriches the human soul. It is nature's love at its best enriched by the merciful love of God.

One example from the Truth and Reconciliation Commission

in South Africa stands out as a shining example of such love.

A policeman recounted an incident when he and other officers shot an eighteen-year-old boy and burned the body. Eight years later he returned to the same house and seized the boy's father. The wife was forced to watch as the policeman bound her husband on a woodpile, poured gasoline over his body and ignited it. The courtroom grew hushed as the elderly woman who had lost first her son and then her husband was given a chance to respond.

'What do you want from Mr Van de Broek?' the judge asked.

She said that she wanted him to go to the place where they burned her husband's body and gather up the dust so that she could give him a decent burial. His head down, the policeman nodded agreement. Then she added a further request. 'Mr Van de Broek took all my family away from me, and I still have a lot of love to give. Twice a month I would like for him to come to the ghetto and spend a day with me so that I can be a mother to him. And I would like him to know that he is forgiven by God and that I forgive him too. I would like to embrace him so that he would know that my forgiveness is real.'

Spontaneously someone in the courtroom began singing *Amazing Grace* as the elderly woman made her way to the witness stand, but Mr Van de Broek did not hear the hymn, He fainted, overwhelmed.

GOING DEEPER

Joseph strived to remain on the way of love all his life. The evidence that he grew in wisdom and stature every day is to be seen in the way he tested the trustworthiness of his brothers and freely forgave them as they embraced their new lives. The goodness and mercy displayed throughout the long life of Joseph truly bore good fruit.

CHAPTER 8

Mercy

The conference was convened in Swanwick by Anglican Renewal Ministries in 1982. Although drained, I was richly blessed by the mutual support and corporate worship of Anglicans reinvigorated by the Pentecostal Renewal. The company assembled was a gathering of those who acknowledged the importance of the outpouring of the Holy Spirit while remaining earthed in Anglican tradition. During an interval I slipped away into the privacy of the chapel for quiet and prayer. Because I was so tired, I found prayer well-nigh impossible but knew I had to be there. I had hardly settled when I saw a vision of myself at six years old. I was sitting on the window ledge of the first floor flat above the cake shop in the village of Writtle, where we moved at the end of the war. My mother had suggested that if I waited there, I might see my father striding across the village green on his way home from the station at Chelmsford – the final leg of his long journey home from India on a troop ship. I was excited at the prospect of his homecoming but nervous because he had been absent for so long. Moreover, I wasn't at all sure that I would recognise him. Caught up in the post-war expectation that things would only get better I couldn't wait to see him. I never saw him walk across the village green. Maybe he wasn't wearing uniform. Maybe I didn't recognise him. Perhaps he came another way. It was then that a dialogue began. It began with a question which took me completely by surprise. There was no audible or imaginary voice, but it was as if the Lord spoke.

'What happened next?'

'I don't know – I can't see.'

I knew I could withdraw from this exchange at any time, but such was the love that I wanted to stay.

'Why can't you see?'

My reply, 'I suppose I was disappointed.'

A further pause and then the final question. 'How did you react?'

I was devastated, for I saw that I had been resentful, bitter and angry. So this was conviction. I didn't feel condemned but bathed and enfolded in God's merciful love. I cannot put into words that sudden awareness of what it means to call God Abba, Father. I didn't feel caged by law but free as a bird. For the next two or three weeks, whenever I was alone I was bathed in tears of sorrow, joy and sadness. This was my baptism of tears which flowed down my face as if a tap has been turned on. My relationship with my father was enriched and I came to a deeper understanding of inner healing. Above all I experienced the patient way God dealt with my sin. Throughout the encounter I knew that I was at liberty to withdraw at any time. Once I had been made aware of what was out of kilter there was no word of correction. I was given space to see for myself. Moreover, I learned that when God convicts of sin, we see the hallmarks of his merciful love. There was no condemnation. To the woman taken in adultery, Jesus said, 'Neither do I condemn you – go your way and sin no more.' This is how it was. This is how it is. I fully understand why it was that Mother Julian of Norwich said that God is not wrathful. Following this encounter, I was left alone to be on my way and to try with the grace of God to sin no more. In 2022, many years after my father died, I had a dream. I was walking down a road crossing the railway bridge at Peterborough station, close to where I hire a car when visiting my family. Coming towards me were my mother and father. I couldn't clearly see my mother, but I knew she was there. My father approached me with a warm smile – not the shy smile I remembered. This was followed by an all-embracing, hug the like of which I never experienced when he was alive.

*

JOSEPH AND JACOB

Joseph was the first born of Jacob's beloved Rachel. Although no Goliath, he was well-endowed and had no problem looking after himself. Further, because of his particular gifts and talents, Jacob was already schooling him to take over when he died. The coat of many colours was a clear statement. Joseph was indeed the favourite. In the years after the brothers returned from Dothan with the blood-stained coat, Jacob lived under a dark cloud, partly because of his loss, and partly because of his unease about the brothers' account of the demise of Joseph. In spite of his dream and vision at Bethel he might have begun to have doubts about the promises to Abraham. Long gone were the blissful honeymoon years with his beloved Rachel, and to make matters worse his favourite son Joseph had been spirited away. In his misery he clung to Benjamin. The veil of grief didn't finally lift until he made up his mind to accept the invitation of Pharaoh to move to Egypt. Freed at last from fear and doubt he prepared to move lock, stock and barrel to his new home. This was to be the first leg of the long journey which was to lead to the promised land.

There is no record of when Joseph finally dealt with residual resentment and bitterness which might have smouldered in the early days of his captivity. Failing to send back news that he was alive in Egypt might suggest that he blamed his father as well as his brothers for his plight. Rather than dwelling on his sufferings, it would seem that he retained a stiff upper lip and pulled down the shutters on his feelings. There was nothing he could do about it so better to keep on carrying on. He worked hard, made good use of his gifts and talents so succeeded in all that he did, and swiftly climbed the ladder of promotion. We don't know exactly when the light of God's merciful love illumined Joseph's heart, opening his eyes not to the faults of failings of which he was already aware and daily addressed, but enabling him to clearly see the canker within, the deep-rooted prejudices and unhealthy attitudes of which he had been previously wholly unaware. There is little doubt, by the kind of man he became, that at some point he experienced this deeper level of forgiveness and inner healing. We know this by the man he became during his years in captivity and by the way he was released from any desire for revenge and cared for his father Jacob, his brothers and their families in Goshen.

RESENTMENT

In Jung and the Christian Way (p.82) Christopher Bryant tells the story of a woman who was very angry with her sister-in-law. As she lay in bed at night, she could not sleep for dwelling on an incident which rankled. She argued the case in her mind and proved to herself that her sister-in-law had behaved abominably. Round and round in her head the argument ran, making sleep impossible. Suddenly, during a pause in her dialogue, she heard a small voice saying *The defendant has admirably made the case for her own prosecution.* It slowly dawned on her that she had behaved in exactly the same way in which she was criticising her sister-in-law.

By the time his father knelt before him Joseph had mellowed. A humbler man, the very idea that he had every right to resent his father or brothers had long since been dealt with. So it was with humility, love and respect that he did all in his power to help his father restore the fractured house of Israel. It can't have been easy for Joseph to have to wait for so long for confirmation that his dreams were true. Nevertheless, because he focussed on God in each present moment, he didn't squander time going round in circles. In the pit he was delivered from the vanity of youth. In prison he was released from complacency. Day by day he was schooled in humility. As Joseph matured it became apparent that he retained a quiet mind during the most troubled times. The peace he experienced was more than the natural peace experienced on a quiet day or while practising mindfulness; Theresa of Avila called such peace *contentos*. The deeper peace, the peace of God, is peace at another level. This she called *gustos*. Such peace cannot easily be disturbed. It is possible to be all over the place while such peace endures. Such is the peace which the world cannot give. It is the very same peace our Lord bestowed upon his disciples before they set out on their costly ministry. Joseph faced a massive upheaval when carted to Egypt. A different land, a different race, a different religion, and yet no-one robbed him of his joy. By the time he saw his brothers and then his father bow down before him he could see that his costly schooling in the Lord's service in Egypt was providential. Over the years the evidence of the kind of man he became leaves little doubt that he became a living prayer and that his soul was robed in the peace of God which passes all understanding; a peace which was infectious and enduring.

*

SELF-RIGHTEOUSNESS

The light of God's mercy enables us to see beyond surface sin. It is more than putting sticking plasters on sores of which we are already well aware. Our blindness allows sinful attitudes, prejudices and the debris of sin to remain embedded within the soul. Such deposits are canker at the core which might remain undetected for a long time before being exposed, addressed and cured. It is such sin about which Jesus speaks when he called the scribes and Pharisees whited sepulchres. Outwardly immaculate but inwardly corrupt. The word used to describe this condition is hypocrisy. A good way to test our hypocrisy is to pay close attention to the way we criticise others. Should we do so we might well find that the things which disturb us most in others are mirror images of our own besetting sins. Pride delights in concealing such truth by making sure that we focus on the short-comings of others. It blinds us to our own failings. It is perfectly possible to be outwardly adorned with the white robes of conformity while being unaware of the unhealthy state of our own soul. I remember a very rough crossing from Harwich to the Hook of Holland on a student trip to the continent on an ecumenical tour. It was impossible to scramble from one deck to another unless pulling oneself up by the handrail. Wind, spray and fresh air, were therapeutic and the deck was the one place one wanted to be. When the storm abated, we gathered for morning prayer. Being the twenty-second morning we read Psalm 107 which included the words, 'These men see the works of the Lord and his wonders in the deep. For at his word the stormy wind arises: which lifts up the waves thereof. They are carried up to heaven, and down again to the deep: their soul melts away because of the trouble. They reel to and fro, and stagger like a drunken man: and are at their wit's end. So when they cry unto the Lord in their trouble: he delivers them out of their distress. For he makes the storm to cease: so that the waves are still. Then are they glad because they are at rest, and so he brings them to the haven where they would be.'

Amen to that fair prayer, I thought. It wasn't just the sea sickness which was no fun. I also suffered from migraine. I was still feeling unsettled when we arrived at Darmstadt. The Marien-schwestern was a community founded and led by Mother Basileia Schlink in response to the sickness in Germany which led to the Second World War. Just before we left after a short stay, a text was placed on every bed. When I first saw mine, I was miffed. Matthew 7 v 1. 'Judge not that ye be not judged.' It wasn't a discreet note handed to me privily by a well-wisher. It was set out along the length of the bed. I wasn't impressed. This wasn't my kind of thing. When I looked it up it hit me amidships. I knew that although I had said nothing, I had been judgemental throughout my stay. Although I never said a word my mind was stuffed with critical thoughts. Although I had reservations about the idea of bearing the sins of a former generation on our own backs when Christ has died once for all I found myself nit picking about everything and getting progressively more and more grumpy. There was so much that was so good which I had over-looked. It was a timely lesson which I have never forgotten. The friend with whom I walked across the paved floor by the entrance as we departed dropped the bottle of communion wine he was carrying. It shattered as the spilt wine streamed across the stone floor between the shards of broken glass. As I look back on that broken glass and red wine it seems to symbolise how careless we are about the treasures of love and mercy to be found in the precious blood of Christ. As a child in the Second World War I learned that many considered every German to be a monster and every British soldier a saint. How different the climate two decades later when I met students at Heidelberg university, when a middle-aged Christian at a dinner told me how important it was that the younger generation never forgot the Nazi scourge.

*

NATURE, NURTURE AND GRACE

There is a natural goodness in Joseph which is to be seen from his early days. At seventeen he goes without question to look for his recalcitrant brothers. In captivity he sought to bring out the best in others. While serving as vizier he encouraged all that was good from the greatest to the least. In Goshen he was a living emblem of God's immeasurable love. Moreover, lessons learned from Jacob and Rachel about the sovereignty of the living God were invaluable. For Jacob surely told Joseph that while wrestling with doubt God intervened. 'And God spake unto Israel in the visions of the night and said, "Jacob, Jacob." And he said "here am I." And he said, "I am the God of thy father; fear not, go down to Egypt, for I will there make of thee a great nation; I will go down with thee to Egypt; and I will surely bring thee up again; and Joseph shall put his hand upon thine eyes."'

The elderly patriarch is filled with joy when Joseph brings his two sons Manasseh and Ephraim to him to be blessed and adopted as his own. While he lived in the land of Goshen, we see the deepening bond between father and son. One day Jacob said, 'God shall be with you and bring you again to the land of your forefathers.' Years later Joseph told his family that he was about to die. Before he died, he asked them to promise to take his bones back home. Centuries later they were taken back to be buried in Schechem but Joseph lives on.

CHAPTER 9

Why Joseph?

Things are not always what they seem. I remember being told as a child that the tiny atoms which constituted the chair on which I was sitting were surrounded by acres of empty space. Archaeologists know very little for certain about the practices of religion before written records, yet it is only necessary to watch seagulls bobbing and weaving in a balletic dance to realise that they are fully aware of what they are doing, where they are going, and why. Some years ago, I watched many hundreds of painted lady butterflies alight on the large sandy beach south of Skegness, knowing that they had no calendar or map yet had found their way from North Africa. There was no need to remind Adam and Eve that what they had done was wrong. Fully aware of what they were up to they hoped to get away with it. Intuitively they knew right from wrong.

When I was about seven years old, I told a silly lie at school to gain attention. Walking home I didn't feel guilty. I wasn't afraid of being found out or punished. Rather, I found myself confronted by the realisation that truth is supremely important. Today I would say that I understood what Christ meant when he said, 'I am the truth.' Truth isn't textual accuracy. It is far greater and more wonderful than all the amazing operations of the little grey cells and transcends the labours of the human mind. Walking home from school that day I suddenly saw that lying of any kind was a slippery slope to be avoided at all costs. Adam and Eve just knew that they were wrong to disobey God. They also knew they were blessed with free will. God made man in his own image. In ways difficult to fathom he has made us so that not only have we been gifted intelligence and free will but retained intuitive gifts shaped from time immemorial. Poets have always known that the world is animated by the spirit of God. As I stood in the shallow water of the beck near the little wooden bridge as a child and looked down through clear peaty water, I knew that it was alive. There was more to it than H_2O. The water was teeming with life. Long before towers, temples or pyramids were erected in Egypt there were things people just knew. Somewhere deep within every man, woman and child there is an awareness that there is something more, someone out there. It begins with Animism. The sense that every little thing from a drop of water to a leaf in the wind is animated by a spirit.

For centuries there was a quest for a universal theory. It was Moses who was made aware that there is one living God who is so far beyond our human understanding and our wildest dreams that he referred to himself as 'I am that I am.' We know that God is God because we see what he does. Because he dwells in light unapproachable, we are unable see him as he is. Nevertheless, one senses that Joseph had always been aware that the hills had been alive with the sound of music and that the sparkling rills were alive. He always knew the material world had a spiritual dimension and even though man might know right from wrong he also knew he had a choice. Joseph must have been aware of this long before his father and grandfather spoke about their theophanies. He imbibed such information with his mother's milk. While climbing the ladder of promotion Joseph displayed moral courage. He didn't allow pride in his success to be his undoing. Unlike King Saul, he never disregarded God or went into a foolish and doomed battle. Nor did he give way to the magnetic pull of lust like King David who, while looking down from his window, saw a beautiful woman bathing naked and seduced her before compounding his fault by placing her husband Uriah in the heat of battle where he lost his life. It is clear that Joseph kept his cool as he would never under any circumstances have murdered another man. Nor like King Ahab would he have been so smitten with envy that he would have lain in bed and sulked all day with his head to the wall, besotted by his desire for his neighbour Naboth's vineyard. From the meagre descriptions we have of Joseph as a young man it seems that he wasn't greedy, didn't overindulge in food and drink, nor did he abuse his body, or misuse his many natural and spiritual gifts. Who knows whether he might have been tempted to throw in the towel while serving an indeterminate prison sentence. In any event he coped by helping the keeper of the prison and taking care of the inmates while containing his soul in patience. I have little doubt that in his claustrophobic cell he was continually doing little things with great love while fending off temptations to hopelessness and despair. Moreover, his life was enriched by virtues priceless in any age – patience wisdom and agape love.

TRIUMPH OVER ADVERSITY

We don't know which Pharaoh or which dynasty was the setting for the ministry of Joseph, but it is generally supposed that it was about 3500 years ago. I can't think of any account from that time which is so well loved as the story of Joseph. Moreover, it resonates with our own. We share his common humanity. Those who first passed on the story knew all about the setting. They were aware of Egyptian customs. They knew about the frequent flooding of the Nile and the consequent recurring famines. Moreover, the story of Joseph is unlike many legends from the past because of the sanctity of the man. It is hardly a pious invention because of its realism. Joseph is so clearly real that the story cannot be reduced to an account of tribal movements. The humanity and individuality of Joseph are as earthed as our own. Further his story highlights the significance of dreams. The joys and sorrows of Joseph speak to us today as if we are separated by a whisker. That there are contradictions in the account in the book of Genesis are a reminder that it passed from generation to generation through story telling before anyone wrote it down. That there are different perspectives is also true. For example, Jacob in mid-life is a very different man from the Jacob who blesses not only Joseph and his sons but the Pharaoh himself. It is clear that, as the story was passed on it matured like a fine wine, enriched by the renewal which emerged from the period after the law book was found by the young King Josiah in the temple. The final flavour belongs to the cask in which the story was preserved before being tapped by the editors of the book of Genesis who encapsulated some of the riches of the spiritual insights of their own time. Given this long history it is hardly surprising that there are inconsistencies. For example, was Joseph sold to traders or taken by Midianites who sold him directly to Potiphar? Such variations have little impact on the overall account. Today, over two thousand years after the book of Genesis was written, how can one fail to be inspired by the story of a man who triumphed over adversity.

I HAD A DREAM

Approaching the end of a long life I am finally beginning to understand the significance of Joseph. First of all, he was called to deliver his family from turf wars in Canaan and take them to a place where they might increase and multiply. Had Joseph not been content to be a slave in an alien land, faithfully serving God, he would never have been in a position to bail out his family during the famine or provide for their future in the land of Goshen. Growing humility helped him to emerge from prison unscathed; humble service to retain his senior position in Egypt. In the panoramic view of my life as a child I was shown that there would be times of trial. In my dream I was directed to Joseph. The ups and downs of his life are inspirational for they demonstrate the value of walking with God through thick and thin. It reminds us that God is with us and in us in trouble and in joy. Joseph has also been my mentor because he wasn't always a saint but became one. There isn't a hint of self-righteousness in the mature Joseph. His love for those whom he served in Egypt was as profound as his love for his own family. The pit was a new beginning. Prison was schooling in the Lord's service. He seems not to have wasted time on regrets but increased in wisdom and stature. When prayer seemed impossible, the whole world against him, and his appeals to his heavenly Father unanswered he remained faithful. He counted his blessings and took care to let no-one rob him of his joy. Good fruit is the evidence that the life of Joseph was steeped in prayer. For Joseph, a living prayer, left in his wake an aura of love and joy. The mature Joseph graciously honoured his father and provided for his brothers. He was real. He was emotional, gifted, sensitive, and underwent a series of crises but never gave up. He was warm, human, and open-hearted.

As I ponder his life story, I see a man who had always known that the world is more porous than many believe. He saw that there is more to the natural world than meets the human eye. He knew that God is not only with us and in us but above and beyond accompanied by the whole host of heaven. Joseph never ceased to have moments when he was suspended in wonder, love and praise at the sheer mystery of it all. What he learned in frequent heart to heart encounters with God shored up his faith. Nor did he forget Jacob's account of the ladder set up from earth to heaven and his night of wrestling with an angel or the words 'Surely God is in this place.' Throughout his long life, faithful Joseph never lost sight of God, whether he was beloved, hated or exalted. In spite of being the victim of hatred, envy and malice he didn't lose his way. The struggle with his ego pulling him this way and that was tempered by his doggedness, fortified by the love and mercy of God. The fullness of his humanity and humility is to be seen when he humbly bowed down to his father. That not a trace of bitterness divided them is demonstrated by his generous and loving response when the sad news came that Jacob was dying. As a youth Joseph had ignored his father's rebuke about his dreams. Later in life there isn't a shred of evidence that he retained a morsel of ill will towards him. Nor is there any evidence of residual bitterness and resentment triggered by the brutishness of his brothers. Day by day throughout his stay in Egypt he worked well with others and became a natural leader who was quietly confident when presented to Pharaoh.

AN INSPIRATION

Almost eighty years after the blackout curtains were removed, I understand more fully why Joseph featured in my dream. His humble acceptance of divine providence was exemplary. From his childhood he was aware of the presence of the living God. Throughout his tribulations he kept his cool. He was principled and studiously kept the ten commandments of Moses long before they were written on tablets of stone. He seems to have known the sermon on the mount and followed its teachings long before they were delivered. Moreover, Joseph always knew that God was with him and in him, whether at home on the farm, being trafficked to a foreign land or while serving for many years in an alien culture, while surrounded by alien religious beliefs. I was inspired by his gifts as a servant leader who knew that the joy of human life is to be found in the loving service of God. His humility enabled him to be flexible and to adapt. Because of his gifts and graces, he became a legend. Had it not been for the insights of the ones who edited the final account in the book of Genesis he might long since have been forgotten. Even as a child I was inspired by the story of a man who walked so closely with the living God and the fact that he lived so long ago was of no consequence.

*

In the 1960s I visited Coventry Cathedral with my parents. The new cathedral stood humbly in the shadow of the ancient bombed-out shell of the old. The art works are remarkable and the Piper windows of particular note. But what struck me most was the richness of treasures, both old and new, standing side by side – the modern building in the shadow of the ancient ruins. Neither have I forgotten words of the preacher at the dedication of the new building. I can still hear Michael Ramsey, then Archbishop of Canterbury, saying, 'There went forth a band of men whose hearts God had touched.' The living church today is planted in well-tilled soil which has been cultivated since long before Joseph was born over three thousand five hundred years ago. Joseph was a way marker on a very long journey across different lands. Jews have called him a second Messiah. Christians have called him an alter Christus. It is difficult to imagine life without Joseph, the star of my dream, whose ultimate desire was to be united with God in both love and purpose. Quite simply to be united in love and purpose with God is the summit of prayer.

CHAPTER 10

The Crucifix on the Wall

In the autumn of 1959, I was working in the Midland bank in Piccadilly in York when one Friday afternoon I was given notice that on the following Monday I was to present myself at a bank in Baker Street in London. Although I had asked for a transfer the short notice came as a complete surprise. I packed my large brown suitcase, took a taxi to York station and found my way to the central YMCA in Great Russell Street. The room cost four guineas a week and basic meals could be purchased in the canteen. Having been paid just two pounds a week when I first worked as an articled clerk this was an improvement, but there was little left from the six pounds a week I was paid by the bank. On the Monday morning, I found my way to Baker Street but was told that I was to go to a branch in Tottenham Court Road – a ten-minute walk from the YMCA.

All was well as I settled down and enjoyed the company of my roommates. This was to be the first step on the road to health, wealth and prosperity, the beginning of a new adventure leading to domestic bliss. I had two roommates: the first moved on to Cambridge and the second was a tuba player from York studying at the Royal Academy of Music. On one occasion, when life seemed drear, on the top floor of the YMCA the three of us, armed with tuba, trombone and saxophone, marched around the encircling corridor on the top floor playing the national anthem, and on another spent an evening busking in Oxford Street raising money for Christian Aid.

All was well for a while as I learned basic banking. There was much that was so good, but as the months passed by, I began to sense that something was missing. I didn't know what it was. The emptiness increased until on my twentieth birthday I awoke in a pall of gloom, knowing that I had lost my way. Midway through 1960 the bedroom door of our room in the YMCA was left open. Roger Harley, who was soon to begin preparing for ordination, noticed the crucifix given to me at my confirmation hanging on the wall above my bed and invited me to serve in the London University church – at that time St Georges Church Bloomsbury. I hesitated because I had never served before so had no idea what to do. There was no time to learn because the service was early the following day. 'Don't worry,' Roger said. 'I will slip a note under your door. This he did. I committed his note to memory and served at the altar for the first time. It was there that I first encountered Father Ivor Smith Cameron.

*

Recently I discovered a book lurking in a corner. It belonged to my mother and might have been given to her in 1934, shortly after her confirmation privately in Bishopsthorpe palace chapel by Archbishop Temple. It was dedicated to Pleshey Retreat House, where I recall kneeling at prayer in the little oratory as a teenager during my confirmation preparation. It was called *The School of Charity*. The following passage is an extract.

The word made flesh and dwelling among us, accepted our conditions and did not impose his. He took the journey we have to take, with the burden we have to carry. We cannot excuse ourselves by saying this is the way we are, this is the way God made us, my faults and failings are only natural, when faced by the demands of the spiritual life. It is as complete human beings taught and led by a complete humanity that we respond to God. The saints carried such burdens. It is no easy amiability which we see transformed to the purpose of creative love in St Paul or St Augustine. George Fox (who after a period of bitter struggle in 1646 discovered moral victory in reliance on the inner light of the living Christ), John Bunyan, the author of *The Pilgrims Progress*, who spent time in Bedford Gaol, knew conflict as bitter as our own. These are they that came out of much tribulation. There are other forms of costly living than martyrdom, many ways of enduring to the end; but none that does not involve the conflict between (complacency in) natural self-love and the supernatural love of God. Grace does not work in a vacuum; it works in the whole man and shows its perfect work in the one of whom we cannot think without the conflict in Gethsemane and the surrender on the Cross. Suffering has its place within the divine purpose and is transfigured by the touch of God. A desperate crisis, the demand for total self-giving, a willingness to risk everything an apparent failure, darkness and death. Those who complain that they cannot pray should examine their capacity for suffering and love. For there is a costly element in the New Testament of which we are warned on every page. This is made ever more apparent as we leave its surface and penetrate its deeps. There we find suffering and love twined so closely together, that we cannot wrench them apart. If we try to do so, the love is maimed –loses its creative power – and the suffering remains, but without the divine radiance of willing sacrifice – so here by the crucifix Christians must test their position. Are we merely to look at it with horror, or accept it with adoration and gratitude, as the soul's unique chance of union with the love of God.

OUR CALLING

What I saw at this time was a unique chance to accept the cross with adoration and gratitude as the gateway to the possibility of union with the love of God. I realised that when Jesus calls us to take up our cross and follow him, he knows us, loves us and has our best interests at heart. He isn't asking us to go in search of suffering for suffering's sake but to be about the business of the one who alone is good. In the third century a number of Christians felt impelled to seek martyrdom. They were, however, discouraged from running head-first into unnecessary confrontation with the authorities. St Cyprian of Carthage himself avoided martyrdom when he could, but a year or two later in his own hometown was awarded the martyr's crown in 258 C.E. Another early account of such courage and humility is Polycarp, Bishop of Smyrna, who did his best not to run into the arms of the authorities. When he was unearthed in his retirement by soldiers to take him for trial his response was profoundly Christian.

First, he asked to be given one hour to pray. Then he ordered a meal to be prepared for the soldiers. When escorted to the magistrate he refused to deny Christ by refusing to burn incense before the statue of Caesar. Affirming his commitment to Christ he said, 'Eighty and six years have I served him, and he has done me no wrong.' Deeply moved, the magistrate tried his best to persuade him to change his mind. Such was his love that Polycarp refused, so was sentenced to death. When Jesus set his face to go to Jerusalem, he knew the risk he was taking. It is unlikely that his family or friends wanted him to set out on such a journey. Imagine the questions. Is this the right way? Is this the right time? Are you sure you know what you are doing? You must be mad! Maybe the response of Mary his mother was to say, 'Do what you have to do.' Following his crucifixion the zealots wrote him off as ineffectual; his disciples ran away; his most faithful supporters were intoxicated by the climate of fear while the crowds drifted home. Only Mary the mother of Jesus and the beloved John stood by the Cross. A crucifix serves as a reminder of the cost of pure love. This is the love in which we are enfolded in heart-to-heart exchanges with our risen living Lord. The spadework is done by immersing ourselves in the witness of Christ and keeping his commands. Prayer is more than a search for tranquillity. Prayer is taking up our cross. For most of us most of the time this doesn't involve heroics but doing little things with great love with ever thankful hearts.

LIGHT AT THE END OF THE TUNNEL

My father-in-law observed that it is often the most unexpected people who carry out the work of God. He wrote, 'This really came home to me recently. I had just lost my wife after some fifty years: I was in fearful torment. I hardly dared to enter a church; I felt so utterly lost and I could not reach any source of comfort. Oh, my children were wonderful, my friends superb, my priest a tower of strength. But somehow, I was cut off, horribly alone, half of myself ripped away; the lovely words of the prayer book had no meaning for me. It was without doubt the most awful and terrifying experience I have known. Then my grandson, a young lad, and one who had himself had a brain injury at birth and who had adored his granny, a beautiful relationship to see, happened to be going to his church. He asked me to go with him and of course I did, because he was not only much loved as my grandson, but also had deep religious conviction, which I could not hurt by a refusal. But then in church, an incredible thing came to pass. He took my hand, just as he used to as a child, only somehow it was as if I was the child, and we knelt together. He put together a simple prayer.

'Please God, help Grandpa.'

As I heard these words, and I cannot explain this – something flowed from my grandson down his arm and into my very soul. The tears came and I wept, and all the time this poor lad afflicted cruelly just held my hand, and smiled such a sweet smile as must have been in the face of Jesus Christ himself. No, I didn't see God; I didn't hear God; I just knew comfort; my faith had returned. (F.E.F. Doubleday *Golden Thoughts* 1989.)

In 1946 we moved to Felsted. While there I suffered from double pneumonia. I was recovering from German measles when my beloved godfather David Bungey visited. We always enjoyed his company, so wearing a dressing gown I was allowed to join the family in the sun porch at the rear of the house. I remember feeling feverish but saying nothing because I was enjoying myself so didn't want to go in. Soon after that the fever raged. One night I found myself floating down a dark bare tunnel in which I could see my immediate surroundings. Eventually I came to a gate. After a pause I found myself on the other side where I was enfolded in an extraordinary sense of well-being, peace and above all love. Blissfully happy, whole and secure in that love, I wanted to remain there for ever. After a while there was a locution. *It's too soon; I want you to go back.* There was no voice, but it was as if the words were spoken. I wanted to stay, and I knew I had a choice. But the divine love in that communication was irresistible. After a pause and a moment for reflection I gave my unspoken consent. As soon as I had done so I felt myself borne back into the world. I awoke. It was 5 a.m. My temperature was 105F. Beside my bed the doctor was standing next to my mother, who still held the thermometer in her hand. Many days were spent half-sitting, half-lying propped up by pillows in bed with a spittoon on the bedside table. I remember coughing and gasping for what seemed to be my last breath. Much of the time I was alone and felt completely detached from the world. I was hardly aware of the comings and goings of the family as they carried on with their daily lives. The whistling of the grocer's boy on his bicycle seemed to come from another world. It must have been 1948 or 1949 because after some time the doctor was able to prescribe M and B (May and Baker), the first antibiotic. Like many who have experienced a near-death experience what I encountered was pure love. Divine love changed my life for ever. I saw a glimpse of the pearl of great price. In spite of wanderings this has been my quest ever since. Death is a glorious new beginning and the material world a miniscule part of reality. I also saw that far beyond our wildest dreams God reigns supreme in all his glory. Far from being a human right every day is a free gift of God to be treasured.

*

It is twenty-one years ago today that I parked on the site of a ruin in Boddam on a glorious sunny day. In spite of the fact that only the walls of the former Earl's Lodge hotel remained I called Susan to tell her that I considered it was indeed the place she had been looking for. She had been called to find a hotel for the hospitality of prayer. It was built by Lord Aberdeen, the first politician to establish the entente cordiale, long before the First World War. It was his retreat and in the following century was occupied by a family member with her Christian community. Seven years after St James House was closed the build was completed and it has been the prayer house called to a ministry of intercession ever since. It was to be a place to regroup and embark upon a very different way of life in another land. The ruin was a call to prayer. While living in a cottage in the village I have been able to support this ministry of prayer and intercession. These twenty years have been years of watching, waiting, and staying at my post. In my study the crucifix hangs on the wall beside me. Both Ivor and Roger died while I was writing this book. Roger also became a priest and served faithfully in the parochial ministry for many years. Ivor had a remarkable ministry and became a chaplain to the Queen. While working as chaplain to IC and surrounding colleges he was responsible for 40 vocations of scientists to the ordained ministry, one of whom I met while speaking to the Ordained Scientists conference a year or two ago. By then he was a bishop, and we discussed the scary experience of crossing London on the back of Ivor's motor scooter. It was Ivor Smith-Cameron who rang me up in the central London YMCA and suggested ordination. I lost close contact with Roger and Ivor many years ago and wonder if either of them realised during their lifetime the way that their moments of inspiration changed the course of my life. I am profoundly grateful. I am also mindful of the importance of not missing God's moments when they come.

Joseph is my mentor. He didn't miss God's moments but treasured them while daily walking hand in hand with God.

Milton Keynes UK
Ingram Content Group UK Ltd.
UKHW042100240924
448733UK00007B/444

9 781789 634839